SELVING

SELVING

Linking Work To Spirituality

William Cleary

Editor

MARQUETTE
UNIVERSITY

PRESS

Library of Congress Cataloguing in Publication Data

Selving : linking work to spirituality / William Cleary, editor.
   p. cm.
Includes bibliographical references.
  ISBN 0-87462-007-4 (pbk. : alk. paper)
  1. Work—Religious aspects—Catholic Church. 2.
Spirituality—Catholic Church. 3. Catholic Church—Doctrines. I.
Cleary, William.
  BX1795.W67 S45 2000
  248.8'8—dc21
                                 00-008319

© 2000 by Marquette University Press
Milwaukee Wisconsin
United States of America

Printed in the United States of America
for Marquette University Press
by Thomson-Shore, Dexter, Michigan, USA

MARQUETTE UNIVERSITY PRESS
MILWAUKEE

The Association of Jesuit University Presses

"The problem of self-identity is not just a problem for the young. It is a problem for all time. Perhaps the problem. It should haunt old age. . . ."

Norman Maclean

"How does identity emerge if not through work?"

Andrew Krivak
(from Chapter One)

CONTENTS

Prelude 9

Andrew Krivak
1. Finding Work 11

Andrew Greeley
2. Forced To Become a Storyteller 20

Rodney J. Hunter
3. Work As Quest 23

Rosemary Ruether
4. From Private Struggle To Public Thought 32

Sarah Maitland
Intermezzo I 35

Raymond A. Schroth
5. Teaching the Self 36

Thomas E. Ambrogi
6. Pilgrim Person On the Road 48

Donna Myers Ambrogi
7. Journeying 57

Rowan Williams
Intermezzo II 64

Charles E. Curran
8. A Spirituality Catholic and Communitarian 65

Robert Blair Kaiser
9. Providence Wore a Jesuit Cassock 77

James Torrens
10. Two Roads Diverged 86

James Carroll
Intermezzo III 94

Wendy Farley
11. Teaching 'Great Books' As Spiritual Practice 95

David R. Blumenthal
12. From Wissenschaft To Theology 102

William F. Powers
13. Journey Without Maps 113

Rumi
Intermezzo IV 122

John Coleman
14. What I Do Is Me 123

William Cleary
15. Dreaming Up a Self 136

Finale 144

Postscript: Honoring Eugene Bianchi 146

Prelude

Selving

The act of "selving" is poet G.M. Hopkins' idea of—and invented word for—the crucial human act. The whimisical image on this book's cover is of the twenty-year old Hopkins looking at himself in a lake, wondering, no doubt, about what kind of man he saw down there, never dreaming he might be sketching a poet to be memorialized by a floor plaque in Westminster Abbey next to Shakespeare, Milton, and Wordsworth. Eighteen years after the cover sketch, he put the same puzzlement into words in the octet of his 1882 sonnet.

As kingfishers catch fire, dragonflies draw flame;
  As tumbled over rim in roundy wells
  Stones ring; like each tucked string tells, each hung bell's
Bow swung finds tongue to fling out broad its name:
Each mortal thing does one thing and the same,
  Deals out that being indoors each one dwells:
Selves—goes itself; *myself* it speaks and spells,
Crying *What I do is me: for that I came.* . . .

This book flows from these words. Hopkins claims that birds, stones, musical instruments—and humans—"deal out that being indoors each one dwells, selves. . . ," and concludes "What I do is me."

The book carries out this "selving" theme. For each of our fifteen narrators, it is an exercise in story theology, working from their own story. They write about their work experiences—their teaching, their writing, their relationships—and identify explicitly or implicitly the tasks that were the most enlivening, the most meaningful—even if they did not succeed. The meaning, the spirituality, proceeded from the work.

We had asked the contributors: write about the thing you've done which you feel came from your inmost self. Identify the times you felt most yourself, most vitalized. What might be your "unique niche of belonging" in the great scheme of things?

Chapter One strikes our keynote. Thereafter, the contributors are all colleagues in some way of Prof. Eugene Bianchi who is now retiring after a lifetime of selving. They add their stories to his in an attempt to celebrate here what, over the years, made their kingfisher selves catch fire.

William Cleary
Winter, 1999

Chapter One
Keynote

FINDING WORK

Andrew Krivak

*A poet finds how work
gives him his meaning*

The road ducked away from South Carolina Highway 17, wound through a trailer park, and disappeared into pines along the Intracoastal waterway. The November, needle-matted ground steamed from the early sun. I drove out of the trees and into a clearing dotted with boats derelict and in dry dock, their prows mustached with the rust of the Waccamaw River. A small shop stood closest to the water, and a long separate shed emerged perpendicular to it at a distance of roughly fifteen paces, extended but not connected, as though together they formed a broken T.

Hague Marina it was called. By some stroke of fortune (though I am unwilling to say whether it was good or bad) I was showing up for my first day of work. I would be paid $5.00 an hour as a laborer in the yard assisting any painters, carpenters or mechanics who needed it, and doing the type of unskilled tasks that boatyards considered "unbillable." Twenty three years old, degree in philosophy, wanting to be a writer more than make a fortune, this was a winter stop I was forced to accept in my self-employed jaunts by boat up and down the coast. Like a traveler stuck in a foreign land, I hunkered down in the South.

Good company welcomed me, though. This was the land of Faulkner, Flannery O'Connor, the tragic West Virginian Breece D'J Pancake, whose stories I loved, and the poet James Dickey (at that time living in Columbia, South Carolina to the west). I'll live and work here, and at night I'll write, I figured. The laborer's work outside on this fecund ground would create its own writer's work inside, and I would find, as Milton said of Adam, "a Paradise within thee, happier far." Perhaps too the work and the men who did it would introduce me to a trade, and I could balance the education by books I had just completed with one I might yet begin with my hands.

I ripped up rotten boards from a diesel dock; the carpenter replaced them. I stripped barnacles and loose paint from the bottom of a trawler; a painter provided the finish. I tore the inside of a sport fishing boat down to its cracked, hull stringers; a shipwright re-fastened her. Mine was an artistry of separateness, or so I told myself for months as I returned day after day to the tedious work placed in my hands because they were hands that could not produce or repair anything. But I must be patient to learn, I resolved. Apprenticeship is as much a matter of time spent as it is skill acquired. I should not expect to do in months what had taken these men years.

Work—real work—is measured in worth. A different time, a different disposition might have allowed me to be content with sweeping up after the men who plied their trades around me. But my questions were rebuffed, my interest and idealism the object of jokes and scorn. That in itself, however, was not impossible to take. My fall came when I realized that these men despised their jobs, hated their work, because in it they only saw toil; in it they could measure no worth, save what money they made. That I might want to learn what they knew made me contemptible, naive, an educated man who would choose to be poor; for that reason I was a fool. With every breath they exhaled their disdain like smoke and invective. Separateness won out over artistry and I began to wither from the acedia of the place.

Then One Day One day in late February the boss asked me to make a delivery in one of the yard's pickup trucks to a local machine shop. The only truck available was one that usually had to be coaxed—bribed almost—into starting. That day, however, she was beyond repair. I walked back into the office to tell the man who'd hired me that the chevy wouldn't start.

"Why aren't you gone?" he asked in his usual insolent tone.

"Truck won't turn over," I said. "I think it's the distributor cap."

"Yeah?" he said. "Well I don't pay you to think. Get another set of keys and get on down to that store."

I just stood there; I didn't feel anger so much as I felt awakened. Then I put the work order on the counter and walked in the direction opposite of where they kept a wall of boat, truck and automobile keys.

"Hey son," he called after me, "where the hell you goin'?"

"I think," I said, "I just quit." And I walked out, half-expecting a hammer or some chrome-plated piece of marine hardware to come sailing through the air at my head. Outside a mean-spirited cabinet maker just hired argued with an awl-grip painter about who should be allowed to begin his job first. I moved past the chevy, its hood still open as though yawning with boredom at the struggles of men, jumped into my car, turned the engine over and drove away.

That's what I wanted to do, but that's not what happened. He did say "I don't pay you to think," and I did stand silently, awakened, but that brief moment in which one believes liberation can only come with a radical and jarring exercise of free will was replaced with the low hum of voices that jockeyed for my attention: the rent check, food, gasoline, repairs on the same vehicle that just moments before promised to get me out of here. The next day I gave my two week's notice, considered the extra $300 (after taxes) a king's ransom, and unheroically left Hague Marina.

In late spring of that year, still longing to do something that was worth the name of "work," I moved to Cape Cod at the prompting of my older brother, and began an apprenticeship of sorts as a yacht rigger at MacDougals' Cape Cod Marine on Falmouth Harbor. There, finally, for what only amounted to a stint of about a year-and-a-half, I can say I worked.

My boss was a bearded, bass-voiced guy who grew up on the North Shore of Massachusetts, spent time in the Coast Guard with my brother, and had moved from the yard across the harbor to MacDougals' as the rigger. His name was Mark Tremblay; he was the best teacher I've ever had. I started with a tool belt of the most basic necessities: screw driver, measuring tape, knife, sockets, pliers, and a small ball peen hammer. Summer was coming on, something of a reprieve time for a rigger. Spring and fall are the high-volume seasons; everyone wants his or her boat in or out of the water. Summer is a time for on-the-spot repairs, tuning, or making up replacement hardware. It took three months to learn my way around the boats, the yard, and the now-growing number of tools I was collecting: splice kits, sail palms and needles, taps and die. I was also watching and being watched by the other men who worked there. No one really said much to me.

What I Learned In those slower summer afternoons, though, Mark took the time to teach me how to splice rope and line; I learned how to swage and nicro-press fittings onto wire; I learned how to measure for, build and install sail furling systems; and I practiced the delicate art of mounting hardware on the water, aloft in a bosun's chair. It were as if Mark believed—remarkably it seemed to me—that in this world of labor, artistry, common sense, and a view of the final product are a man's three greatest natural resources. Four, if you include a pair of hands.

When fall came and the summer help went back to school, I stayed. I was sure I was getting sized up as just another kid who wouldn't last a season. Decommissioning season begins in mid-September. Each day is a constant drill of disassembling boats, storing masts, making notes of needed repairs for work in the winter. There is little opportunity for artistry but much demand for common sense.

I won't romanticize the place; boatyards are no way to make a fortune. Yet more than geography separated this boatyard from the one at which I'd worked in the South. On the Cape I lived within a culture of boats. Men were respected for what they knew about boats, and they sought specialties in engine repair, electronics, or rigging just as a physician would choose an area of medicine or a lawyer an area of law. And from these men, with some of whom I had only an employer in common, I learned what work is; not what lucrative work is, but what meaningful work is. The difference between the so-called work I had done at Hague Marina and the work I was doing here was clearer to me than open water. It was the difference between toil and creativity.

During Christmas of that year I took a week off and went out to California to visit my sister. After New Year's I came back to work, walked into the office where they kept the time clock, punched it, and heard my name drawled out with a downeast accent. One of the haulers, a slow-moving but decisive Vineyarder who had been working on boats, asked me how my holiday was. I turned around to see if he was really talking to me, so accustomed was I to walking into that room every morning invisible or ignored, never speaking to anyone. He waited for me to answer. I told him it was a good one, that I enjoyed the time with my sister and her husband, but that California could be pretty damn cold in December. "Not like here," he said. "Been colda' than a well digger's ass." I laughed. "But I'm glad to be back," I added as casually as possible, retreating into a long sip of coffee. "Glad to have you back," he said, and fairly ghosted out the door into January.

After a year and a half at MacDougals', I left the boatyard for a writing program in New York City. Given the relatively short length of my stay, I cannot say properly that I learned the rigger's trade. Still, as though he knew that I would serve and be served better in a world where words were the stock on which I worked, my boss and teacher supported the decision, said I would probably write no matter how I drew my pay, but that doing one thing full time, if you loved it, was the only way to justify getting out of bed every morning.

I remember that last day. The yard manager gave me a check for an amount I would have accumulated had I been given a raise in pay; my brother, also a rigger, presenting finger-less gloves to me in August, joked that I'd need them in the winter to hold subway tokens just as I'd used finger-less gloves here to free shackles and bolts when it was freezing; then, in the afternoon, Mark, my brother and I took a boat we'd been working on out for a sail, checking its tuning like a mechanic checks an engine's timing; then we just let her cruise.

Defining Work   What is work that it might give meaning to both the rigger and the writer, the builder and the poet? Work that is productive or creative is not necessarily work that strives for some prelapsarian perfection. Work, the author of Genesis assured, is not the curse of the fall - "sweat" is. Work is what brings us back to an understanding of ourselves and our relationship with God. For, in the "tilling" (avodah in the Hebrew) of the "ground" (adamah), Adam finds in that ground his name, his very self.

Catholicism understands work as a restorer of dignity after the shame of the sin. The dignity of work rests in its capacity to effect an imitation of Christ, the new Adam. Work is not what we do for salvation, but rather how we might come to understand salvation. We work our earthly *adamah*, often in suffering, as Christ worked the ground of our salvation so that suffering would be no more. Vatican Council II entreated "those who engage in human work, often of a heavy kind," to "perfect themselves through it to help their fellow citizens, and promote the betterment of the whole of human society and the whole of creation.... [T]hey should imitate Christ who plied his hands with carpenter's tools and is always working with the Father for the salvation of all." For this reason, work defines the human person. It is a duty that "honors the Creator's gifts and the talents received from Him." And it is redemptive, "a way of animating earthly realities with the Spirit of Christ."

When work is simply toil, however - that is, when the person becomes a means to an end that may only tangentially (if at all) serve him —work is a fragmented, unredemptive task. In what Marx called "alienated labor," the worker whose labor is seen only as a commodity moves through four moments of increasing separation from product, activity, community, and finally the self. In his metaphor of the lord and bondsman, Hegel asserted that, although the lord is in a position to be feared, his idleness creates a spiritual poverty, while the bondsman through work grows in skill and knowledge, not just of the task at hand but of his own self. Through work one becomes conscious of who one truly is.

The Protestant Twist   The Protestant work ethic, which has its roots in the Reformation belief that a layman's work could be as holy as the monk's, adds a moral twist to what would be the fruits of labor. A man who works receives wealth, a blessing or favor from God. A man who labors a great deal and still strains under the yoke of poverty is not so much caught in a dynamic of class as he is guilty of some sin that has not yet been brought to light; it is manifested in the labor that affords no blessing of wealth, and presumably never will. With that twist we see work's darker underbelly. The poor are not just those whom we will always have with us. Rather, in this calculus of morality and labor, the poor may not be favored by God for reasons only they and their creator know.

The Roman poet Virgil, far from the philosophy and theology of modernity, called it *labor improbus* in his poem the *Georgics*: damned hard work. It is humankind's contract with existence that "stands unchanged / Since Deucalion threw stones into the empty world / And men rose up and entered on their hard lives. / To work then!" Virgil believed that the Roman empire crumbling in his time suffered as much from "the countryman ignorant of the land he works," as it did from political and moral dissolution. It is not the strength of an empire that determines what an acre of land or a flock of sheep are worth. Rather, what the land yields and what a flock of sheep are worth is what determines the worth and strength of the empire. When pruning hooks are "beaten into swords," and "the plough dishonored," the empty fields portray a moral as well as agrarian waste. Had The Georgics been simply a handbook for farmers, it would be unknown today. Virgil survives, I think, because The Georgics is as much a poem about poetry as it is about vines and animal husbandry. Virgil used the metaphor of work to write about his own work, the work of making, the work of *poietes*. He does that damned hard work damned well.

In the last book Norman Maclean wrote before he died, *Young Men and Fire*, he tells the story of fifteen US Forest Service Smokejumpers in Montana, who in 1949 faced a wall of fire moving up a hillside with the speed of a train. Twelve died in mid-stride; two outran the blowup; one survived by laying down in a fire of his own making, giving the fire in pursuit nothing on which to feed. Maclean knew the Forest Service, he knew the forest in Montana, and he knew fire. When he takes up the subject of work, he too is motivated by the shared experiences of work and "making." When Maclean writes of work his is writing about self-identity.

In notes discovered after his death, Maclean wrote that "the problem of self-identity is not just a problem for the young. It is a problem all the time. Perhaps the problem. It should haunt old age, and when it no longer does it should tell you that you are dead." He grappled finally with the question—a writer in old age—by telling the story of "young men whose lives I might have lived on their way to death." Like Virgil, Maclean seems almost duty bound to tell this story about the work of others, to tell it well, and to find at the heart of the "making" his very self.

How Identity Emerges And how does identity emerge if not through work, through disparate tasks somehow productive, failed attempts - sometimes mortally - that possess some generative meaning, and finally the awareness that we are not the task or trade, but the gradual unfolding of a person. Creation is a process, ground continually turned under; meaning rests in the making as much in what has been made. Perhaps only this can be said about work: that it is the story of our becoming, even as it draws us toward our end.

Once on a visit to the Cape, I dropped in on Mark, my boss from MacDougals'. He doesn't work on the harbor anymore, and he and his wife have moved into a house with land that fronts a river. I caught him just about to row out to retrieve a raft that had gotten loose in a late season storm, and was hung up on a sand bar where Perch Pond opens to Vineyard Sound. "I could use the help," he said, so I climbed aboard the small lithe skiff he was going to use for the towing. The tide was ebbing; the ride back, attached to a raft of boards and Styrofoam floats, would be work. I practiced some knots while we caught up on our lives; the sky blanketed us with a light rain. When we got to where the raft was, we saw that eel grass had kept the pontoons out of the sand, so it would be easy enough to drag. I tied the near side off to a line crossing the stern of the skiff in a bridle, then stepped up and through a rotten board. "It's repairable," he said, and I wondered whether he meant the raft or me. He tugged twice to swing the bow around, motioned me back in, then began slowly drawing the hulk from its rest.

As we rowed back, I thought about those days when I was the rigger's apprentice, where I learned the importance of the knot. That worked derived a certain order and meaning from the wrap, tuck and cinch of line against line to stand, tow, trim and set. I have searched for that order within me. I've watched storms release moorings, push others back to shore, the whims of nature's antagonists and intercessors battling against each other in their own work of retrieval and of loss, and still my work becomes this: Under icy water I anchored that raft—a vessel I possess only in its retrieving—again to the place from which it had broken free, my hands tightening each shackle to the submerged, rusting chain. Then, secured, tested, trusting what strength we had given it, he decided to keep that beat-up wooden raft another season.

(*Andrew Krivak is a poet and essayist. His first collection of poetry,* Islands, *was published by the Slapering Hol Press in Fall 1999. He is currently a doctoral student in English Literature at Rutgers University. This essay first appeared in* The Boston College Magazine, *Spring 1999. Used with permission.*)

Chapter Two

FORCED TO BECOME
A STORY TELLER

Andrew Greeley

*A novelist is born
from sociology*

I was trained in the seminary to reflect on religion from the top down—from dogma and theology down to practical pro grams—and learned in the parish of Christ the King to work with religion from the bottom up—from human problems and needs to religious responses. Sociology taught me to reflect on religion from yet a third perspective: from the empirical experience of the sacred to the articulations, imaginative and propositional, by which we try to share our experiences with others and to represent them to ourselves.

I began to comprehend, slowly at first, from my study of religion and ethnicity that religion was storytelling before it was much else and that ethnicity was, in the United States, the locale for most religious storytelling.

Sociology forced me eventually to become a storyteller. . . .

My thinking about symbols was heavily influenced by three writers, Mircea Eliade (whom I had read even before graduate school and from whom I had taken a reading course at the university), Michael Polyani, the philosopher of science, and William James, the greatest of American thinkers, whom Santayana properly described as "an Irishman among the Brahmins." From Eliade I learned that there were certain fundamental structures of religious experience and expression which seemed almost universal, even though they manifested themselves in dramatically different forms. . . .

While reading Eliade's *Patterns of Comparative Religion* I had my first insight that Mary's functional role in Catholicism was to reflect the womanliness of God, a development from, not the same thing as, the female deities in the nature religions. . . .

From Polyani I learned that human knowledge did not follow the paradigm of the "scientific method," a confirmation of the way I observed myself and other sociologists working. We followed instinct, hunches, intuitions, much like a detective solving a mystery story. All our "method" did was provide us techniques for experiments which would prove what we already knew to be true—perhaps refining our intuitions in the process. The so-called conflict between scientific and religious knowledge evaporated in the light of Polyani's understanding. Subsequently, reading about the work of theoretical physicists (like the remarkable Stephen Hawking) I realized that on the frontiers of science men worked with symbols, myths, models and stories, much as did the searchers for religious truth.

Then James taught me that *all* quest for truth was an exercise in model fitting, a conclusion to which the cognitive psychologists were coming in the early seventies—and in the process rediscovering the genius of James. We fit our explanatory schemes (models, narratives, symbols, culture system, whatever we choose to call them) to the reality we experience and then modify the explanations to make them better fit reality. Knowledge is an empirical, pragmatic exploration through mystery. James's criteria—luminosity, congruence, and fruitfulness—were merely an empirical description of how the human mind worked. . . .

I had, then, by 1970 the raw materials for my paradigm of religion—experience, symbol (image) story, and community—which would in later years shape my sociology (and become my principal contribution to the field) and give the impetus to my storytelling. The success of my stories would doubtless satisfy greatly the empirical, pragmatic William James. That success fitted perfectly the model of religion I had constructed. . . .

from *Confessions of a Parish Priest* (Simon and Schuster, New York, 1986, p. 222). Used with permission.
***

There have been three turning points so far in my life as a priest. The first was in the early sixties when I took the Sunday Night Group at its word and embraced the ideal of professional competence over against clerical mediocrity. The second was in the middle seventies when my socioreligious reflections led to a paradigm which emphasizes the imaginative, the poetic, the communal, the traditional, the nonpropositional aspects of religion. The third was in the late seventies when, impelled by the momentum of the first two turning points, I began to try to write stories of God.

I resolved to be the best I possibly could at what I was doing. As I studied the response not only of the intellect but of the whole personality to religion, I told contemporary parables. All three were unexceptionable activities, until they were marked with the tainted word "successful."

Each of the turning points brought me farther down the road. It is impossible to go back, even if I wanted to.

I wrote previously, perhaps too militantly, that my terms are acceptance and freedom. Realistically, I don't expect acceptance. Realistically too I don't expect freedom unless I'm prepared to fight for it whenever someone tries to mess with me.

Could it ever be otherwise? I don't see how, but as I said in the beginning of this story, I don't believe in burning bridges.

It ought not to be this way. As a friend remarked at supper the other night, any priest who does anything will be in trouble with his fellow clergy. No priest should have to endure from his fellow priests what those of use who try to do something today have to endure. Okay, I survived, but no thanks to the clergy.

The Church cannot continue to permit the priesthood to impose on its members the lowest common denominator of envy-ridden, passive/aggressive mediocrity. The Church will not be able to respond to the challenges and the opportunities of the years ahead without a sophisticated, professionally trained, mutually supportive, enthusiastic clergy.

That too, I fear, is for the decades, the centuries. . . .

(ibid. p. 499)

(*Andrew Greeley is a best-selling novelist, a sociologist by profession, and a Roman Catholic priest and pastor.*)

Chapter Three
WORK AS QUEST

Rodney J. Hunter

*A spirituality emerges
in seminar settings*

For better or for worse, work has never been anything for me but a spiritual quest, a fact that makes me a rather odd academic I suppose. I chose to become a pastoral theologian (a field not readily explained but related to the analysis and interpretation of religious care in relation to personal need (because it seemed like the best vehicle for exploring certain kinds of questions that grasped me both as intellectual problems and as personal, even perhaps pathological, certainly existential, issues.

I wanted to know, for instance, how the mysteries of human personality that I had begun to explore in seminary studies with Seward Hiltner could illuminate or otherwise clarify theological questions that has long puzzled and fascinated me. Where does our sense of "God" come from? How can we sift out the pathological from the trustworthy in religious feelings and beliefs? What must I do to be saved?

I got my first insights into possible answers as I plunged into graduate study and later, clinical pastoral education. My questions changed in certain ways, but it never seriously occurred to me that the pursuit of pastoral theology (or "personality and theology" as it was called at Princeton Seminary (could be anything but a quest for Truth—certainly not a career in the ordinary sense. I felt mild contempt for graduate students who seemed not to seek the truth of their disciplines with the same ardor, the same idealistic dedication as myself. And frankly, this romantic idealism has never left me, though it has undergone a chastening and, I like to think, a maturing through the fires of several major projects.

Bedside Experiences   The first instance, I suppose, was my experiences in clinical pastoral education(a trial by fire in mental and general hospitals for a year and a half where I tried to bring fullness of life, or at least the consolations of real presence, to the bedsides of people suffering in terrible ways that I myself had never known and still have never known. In my twenties, in good health, eager and grandiose about my aims and future, I listened to their stories and their anguish as best I could. I had many deep and memorable experiences with some of them, a little boy bravely enduring in a cage of stainless steel around his head till his little body finally gave out, a young mother grieving the sudden death of her two sons on an electric tower, a dazed teenage boy whose entire family had just been killed on Interstate 75 next to the hospital, a woman fighting for her life with mounting despair against the crushing pain of one of this nation's early heart transplants.

My boat of faith got badly tossed under the impact of these experiences, and toward the end of that training I came close to abandoning my commitment to pastoral theology altogether. Yet I somehow summoned a resolve that steadied my compass and led me back to the academic dimension of my graduate studies, determined to do something in my dissertation that might make a really worthwhile contribution to the world of psychological and theological meanings. Ultimately I hoped to help the church and ministry that seemed to me had been profoundly shaken by the rise of "psychological consciousness," though they were perhaps too seduced and dazed by it to realize what was happening.

I returned to Princeton from my hospital experiences, and plunged into something of a bizarre intellectual project. Ordinary dissertation topics would not do; simple academic labor for a degree was beneath contempt. My aim was higher. I would tackle what I considered to be the most fundamental pastoral theological question facing the church and its ministry. Just before my clinical work I had read Philip Reiff's magnificent book, *The Triumph of the Therapeutic*. Rieff advanced a polemical thesis about the subversive impact of Freud and psychoanalysis on the way western people internalize culture.

He argued that psychoanalytical insight had weakened internalized social control and given individuals an unprecedented inner liberation from the inner compulsion of culture. Into that thesis I thought I could read precisely my own story and that of my generation. And I could see there too how the entire field of pastoral theology was itself one of the chief purveyors of this radically new, psychological form of human consciousness to the churches. With a profound sense of urgency that I suppose constitutes a therapeutic equivalent of the old religious sense of calling, I set about to construct a theoretical reply to Rieff. My calling was to show that commitment in all forms and expressions of human social engagement is still possible and still a moral good in human affairs, though a good bit humbled and substantially revised by the considerations elaborated in Rieff's thesis of the new psychological culture.

Commitment was hardly a term in professional or academic use in 1968. There were few psychological studies of it, and those I found were mostly in sociology and social psychology, neither of which at the time seemed terribly relevant or helpful to my psychoanalytic interests (though since then I have come to hold the diametrically opposite opinion). I struggled with the problem of how to set up a dissertation that would construct both depth psychological and theological accounts of personal commitment, each critiquing and contributing to the other, that would also look like a bona fide academic research study.

After an agonized year of struggle and false starts, I finally worked up a defensible if unconventional research method, an elaborate scheme that involved extracting constructive implications from the theories of Freud, Rogers, Pannenberg, and the biblical covenant tradition, and constructing both psychological and theological theories of the "act of personal commitment" from them.

University Appointment A faculty appointment at Emory University happily entered the picture at this point. The challenge and joys of teaching full time for the first time was both stimulating and distracting, but the weight and complexity of the dissertation, and the ever expanding time it required, put me under a terrifying pressure as I began to fantasize about the possibility and consequences of failure. But two years and 587 pages later I had at lest some of my theoretical answers as well as a degree and a life-changing marriage commitment as well. But oddly enough I never regretted the travail of this idealistic quest. My dissertation was a deeply important creative experience for me for which I learned ineffable lessons about questing and sacrificing and aiming high. And through it I fashioned most of my concepts about what it means to do theology authentically, as an existential as well as an intellectual task. In later years I have discovered the dangers in this romanticism as well, for myself and especially for my students, for whom I perhaps too readily wish a similar depth and passion of engagement

It may be a flaw in my nature that this project failed to cure me of such spiritual questing through academic research. Within six years of completing my degree, now well advanced in teaching, even tenured, I found myself once again smitten by the Great Work demon. In late 1980 I become general editor of an encyclopedic reference volume that soon became a consuming passion and very nearly consumed me in the end. The *Dictionary of Pastoral Care and Counseling*, to which alone my professional obituary will most likely refer, appeared on the scene as a creative intellectual opportunity at a time when no comprehensive reference work existed in pastoral theology.

The field had burgeoned and proliferated in the years since. Counseling and all of the psychological interests related to it had swept the churches and become established in the Protestant seminaries, and had spawned two new religious professions in less than a quarter century (clinical chaplaincy and pastoral psychotherapy). Therapies and theories of personality abounded in a cacophony of competing voices, each with its advocates in the secular world and its disciples in the churches. The churches' historic caregiving traditions and rituals were pronounced of no use; theology seemed irrelevant to "helping people." New professions, institutions, and careers had sprung into existence around these developments.

Here in the *Dictionary* project (which was always more nearly an encyclopedia than a dictionary) I saw my chance to do another Great Work, one that would contribute far beyond my own happiness to the great enterprise of ministry itself. It was an opportunity to sort this mess out and give a new, clear, historically and theologically informed definition to psychologically oriented ministry, to critique and critically appropriate the welter of psychologies and therapies that vied for the church's adoption, and to construct a new, comprehensive vision of church and ministry that would carry forward the critical engagement with depth psychology in contemporary western religious life and ministry.

The *Dictionary* was indeed an immense if not grandiose undertaking, and quickly grew to monster proportions. My editors and I slogged through mounting, unanticipated months of planning and decision making that constituted the conceptual heart of the project, then labored for years and years putting the plan into effect. Stacks of problematic manuscripts flooded in from well meaning academics and clinical authors who frequently had good insights but little concept of what it took to write in the interdisciplinary, theory-praxis genre of pastoral theology. Creative editorial opportunities appeared at every turn, however, and I found myself repeatedly thrilled with the possibilities of conceiving articles on significant new or forgotten topics and interrelating them through a massive system of cross references (on 3x5s, just before the advent of the PC), as well as revising and redrafting the often conceptually limited manuscripts we received.

Here again, for me, work and destiny somehow flowed together. Once again I had become committed (the theme of my life(to a work that was also a mission, a calling, and ultimately, after sometimes terrifying travail, a profound and sublime fulfillment. The book, which involved the sacrificial labors of many others as well as myself, was finally published by Abingdon Press in 1990, ten years from its inception.

Most of my academic writing has imbibed a similar spirit of intellectual and spiritual quest. I often grappled with complicated interdisciplinary problems and I have never been greatly interested in writing conventional academic pieces. And while I cannot boast of great publishing achievements with any of these essays, looking back I see this theme of intellectual-spiritual quest running through them like a thread of fate if not a compulsion. And the future looks no different.

Devotion To Teaching But I write as if research and writing were the heart and sole of my work, when in truth most of my work and energy over the past twenty eight years at Emory University has been devoted to teaching, to the point where my self esteem as a publishing faculty member has felt at times threatened by my relatively sparse though intense bibliography.

I have never adequately resolved, either pragmatically or in principle, how best to proportion my time and energy between teaching and research. It's a problem for me. Consumed by teaching and students and program needs on a daily basis, like every faculty person I have felt driven by the conflicting pressure and desire also to write. I disdain colleagues who quietly cheat their students by failing to supervise and honestly critique their work or to become involved in the personal meanings of their educational experience. If anything I make myself too available to students who need to explore, process, and sometimes just suffer together with me.

But I also pity teachers who fail to extract themselves from the immediacies of student and institutional life. Indeed, one of the most fascinating and persistent moral issues of my life has been the struggle between private and public goods, between the nurturing of student minds and hearts on one hand, and research and writing for a wider world of scholarship on the other; between family and profession; between institutional duty and private pleasure. And I wonder: does human fulfillment favor one over the other? Are public careers and achievements necessarily of greater or more enduring worth than the intangible, invisible, private values of a friendship cherished and enjoyed, or a pastoral counseling relationship that moves profoundly toward healing and hope, or a moment of illumination in the liturgy, or of contemplative ecstasy, or the joy of an authentic intellectual insight? My instincts lean toward the latter.

I do know, however, that some of the grandest experiences of my professional life have been in the classroom, especially in seminar settings which seem to be my forte, and in long conversation lunches with colleagues and graduate students. I savor vivid memories of illuminating discussions of complex and deep things that seemed like very heaven, and a few classes that would not end even after I called time and tried to leave. What matters to me about such experiences is, I think, less the ego strokes they give than the elation of participating in a process of reflection and inquiry that seems to transcend practical considerations and egoistic needs. The search for truth, a much despised concept in academia today I fear, burns bright within me in these situations. Perhaps it is slightly delusional or platonic to think so, but for me the ideal of the academy as a community of scholars devoted to the truth is not without experiential meaning or possibility. I strive in every class to enable students to rise above cynicism, distraction, and myopic utilitarian attitudes to enter into the spirit of inquiry and reflection, the true work of education.

For me education entails entering the great stream of human culture regardless of subject matter, participating in an activity that must surely rank among the great ends of human life. Of course, the classroom should be a human *community*, and academic life should also be humane, caring, charitable, and just. It is important to me that my students feel known, respected, and personally called into the work of the mind with me. But fundamentally the classroom should be a sacred space and time. Teaching and learning involve a mutual quest for that which is true and good, the making as well as transmitting of culture, and the formation of truly civilized as well as faithful and good human beings. Education at its best is a moral and spiritual enterprise.

Forming My *Self* I suppose I would be less than truthful were I to end this extravagant self reflection without touching briefly on another spiritual theme that runs through every aspect of my work. Raised a good Presbyterian with a healthy superego and a passion for "righteousness," I have always found it difficult to accept students and other academic who fail to care deeply about the quality of what they do. I can tolerate, accept, and help students with serious academic deficiencies without hesitancy, and I do a lot of essentially remedial "charity" work with such students. But with them as with the others, taking care to do things well, whatever one's limitations and capacities, is one mark of authentic personhood and moral character, despite the risk of an unreasonable perfectionism.

I am aware of the social and historical relativity and possible obsolescence of this quaint romantic conception today. But it is a deeply resonant with me. It is also a demon to contend against, and I strive (with frequent lapses) to stay just this side a compulsive perfectionism. Yet I remain committed to the moral and spiritual importance of trying to do worthwhile things *well*, and letting the chips fall, in the hope that some redeeming grace will emerge in the process to save me from myself and restore my work to its rightful proportions. Forgiveness, grace, and freedom are themes close to my heart as might be imagined of one so committed to *being* committed. I will spare the reader more intimate reflections on the way these issues have woven their bright and somber threads through my life, and through my work and calling as a theological educator, except to say that work has always provided me the great testing and questing ground for these spiritual tensions. My work slips into *works* in the theological sense, a condition that sooner or later exhausts my good will and frustrates the work itself, driven as it by that quiet, understated threat of shame that terrorizes academics with the thought of real failure in the eyes of their colleagues. Work truly entails a curse, or at least a potential curse, for Protestant types like me, and I must be reminded over and over, by folks like, for instance, long time colleague Gene Bianchi, that the measure of my soul exceeds, in worth and in being, the things I do.

In this connection I am in fact reminded of the colleague we are honoring in this volume. Gene is one of those rare spirits in my academic experience with whom I have felt a truly gracious presence, a perspective on life that is not entrapped in the narrow competitive values of the academic zoo, and the kind of courage and honesty to raise an eyebrow when I begin waxing a bit too serious about the great things I may be trying to accomplish. Gene is not opposed to striving, but I hear in him deeper tones that I envy and would gladly find in myself, tones that seem in tune with a inner sense of goodness at the heart of things that abides however much, we storm the heavens with our ambitious designs, and that welcomes us into the dance of life however much we succeed or fail.

In my own theological tradition I find it useful to remind myself that a life of committed work, like a life of committed anything, can thrive, or even in the long run survive, only when it lives from a Source of freedom and grace deeper and more encompassing than itself. I don't know what the larger scheme of things may involve which the petty struggles of this romantic academic may fit into. But I do sense that trying to do a few worthwhile things well, and trusting in the grace of life regardless, must be a good part of what it's finally all about.

(*Rodney J. Hunter, a professor at Emory University, is general editor of the* Dictionary of Pastoral Care and Counseling *and co-editor with Pamela D. Couture of* Pastoral Care and Social Conflict [*Abingdon, 1995*]).

Chapter Four

FROM PRIVATE STRUGGLE TO PUBLIC THOUGHT

Rosemary Ruether

*A feminist scholar discovers
her authentic call*

To be more and more fully alive, aware and committed, this is surely the meaning of a journey of faith. But this must mean that we are always reassessing and re-appropriating the past—our own past experiences and reflections—in the light of new challenges. A side journey in our spiritual progress, one temporarily shelved, might suddenly become urgent again. In the light of new cultural demands, one might have to look again at some apparently closed question from one's past to see what is usable. . . . There is a hermeneutic circle with our own past experiences and thoughts, just as with the historical past. What our past means at any given time is always conditioned by the present questions that we bring to it. . . .

from *Disputed Questions: On Being a Christian* (Abingdon, Nashville, 1989, p. 14).

***

It is not surprising that as I personally began to move from private struggle to public thought, one of the first areas I chose to write in was sexuality and reproduction. A major effort was needed to break open the closed Catholic culture on birth control. Although I had been working out my private dissent for some years, an incident in the maternity ward where I had given birth to my daughter Mimi in 1964, galvanized my criticism on the subject.

In the next bed there lay a Mexican-American woman named Assumptione. She had just given birth to a ninth child, born with the cord wrapped around its head. The doctor came to her bedside frequently to report the progress of the child, but also tactfully to recommend that she not return home without some adequate means of contraception.

Tearfully the woman described to me the impoverished conditions into which she would take this ninth child to join its eight brothers and sisters. The house was without central heating. She had to turn on the stove to keep the place warm and was always in terror of being asphyxiated by the fumes. There was little food. Her husband beat her. But, when urged to take some measures against a tenth pregnancy, she could only reply that her priest did not allow her. Her husband also was against it.

She also told me *that her umbilical had hurt* during the pregnancy, and she was afraid that the cause was that the child had the cord around its neck. I realized with horror that this mother of nine children had no clear understanding of her own physiology. She did not even know that her own umbilical was not connected to that of the child.

This incident precipitated my private struggle and dissent onto the public plane. It became evident that the church's position on contraception was a public crime causing untold misery in millions of lives throughout the world, among people far less able to defend themselves that I. It was necessary to criticize this policy and the entire sexual ethic and viewpoint on women and marriage that it represented, not just for my own sake, but for those millions of Assumptiones weeping in maternity beds around the world.

So my first feminist writings of the midsixties focused on the criticism of the Catholic views of sexuality and reproduction. Only gradually did it become clear that these views themselves were an integral part of a sexist ideology and culture whose purpose was to make women the creatures of biological destiny. This was connected not only with woman's reproductive role, but her work role in the household and in the society. . . . (*ibid.* p. 117)

***

My account of my personal and religious journey entails many negations as well as affirmations. Unless the relationship of the affirmations to the negations is rightly understood, much of what I have said will be misconstrued. Some will say, "Why be a Christian if Christianity has been anti-Semitic, politically oppressive, and sexist?" Or others will say, "You are not a Christian if you criticize these things."

There are two ways to criticize things, an oppositional and a dialectical way. The oppositional way simply sets up an affirmation as a repudiation of its opposite. The good socialist is set up against the bad capitalist; the good feminist against the bad sexist, and so on. . . .

I would regard my own mode of thinking as dialectical. I see negation, not as an attack on someone else's person or community, but as a self-criticism of the distortions of one own being, of one's own community. Criticism of these distortions opens up the way for a positive reconstruction of the healing and liberating word of the tradition. . . . This is the healing and liberating word that I have heard emerge from the Christian tradition, once freed of its distorted consciousness. This is the healing and liberating word I would hope to communicate to others.

But this healing and hope is available only through the cross of negation. This cross of negation means both theoretical struggle against false ideologies of oppression and practical struggle against its social consequences. Only through this struggle does one hear a healing word and glimpse an alternative future. . . . (*ibid.* p. 141

(Rosemary R. Ruether is a prolific author and columnist, a professor at Garrett School of Theology, Evanston, Il. The citations are used with permission.)

Intermezzo I

Selves. . .

COMING INTO BECOMING. . .

God calls on us to be grown-ups, and
fellow workers, offering us a difficult
but exciting task—creating one
another's humanity. Freud speaks to
this understanding: the language we
use, the bodies we have and the ways
we act, especially towards children
but continuously towards each other,
is mutually self-creating. It matters
what we do. Persons, selves, are continually coming into becoming in our
every act. . . .

Sarah Maitland in *A Big-Enough God*

Chapter Five

TEACHING THE SELF

Raymond A. Schroth

*A teacher's spiritual outlook is shaped
by students' struggles*

As a Jesuit scholastic in 1962 I took a graduate English course in the educational philosophy of John Henry Newman at Fordham from the renowned Francis X. Connolly, a Catholic poet, editor of an influential anthology, *Literature, the Channel of Culture* (1948), who believed, as many did then, that literature was a guide to a good life, and he weighted his book with writers like Maritain, Newman, and Thomas Merton, who shared the Christian worldview. For Newman (I wrote in my term paper), the relationship between student and teacher is an intellectual friendship, where for truth to live in the student, "he must catch it from someone in whom it lives already."

***

I don't think that is the first thought in the minds of the wenty students in my Fordham freshman English course, Close Reading and Critical Writing, the first day of class, January, 1999. Nor in mine.

I am laying down rules—no food, no water bottles, no gum, no absences or lateness, no late papers (not even one minute), no book

bags on the desk, no hats, no stacking books before the class is dis-
missed—all meant to drive home the idea that literature is extremely
important, that the work we are doing together demands every atom
of our concentration. For the first time in many years, to force myself to break from familiar material I've taught before, I've put myself
at the mercy of a standard textbook, *Elements of Literature*, chosen:
because it includes essays, fiction, poetry, drama, and film; because it
is not divided into artificial categories like "stories about family life,
etc."; and because it has none of those "questions for discussion"
after each piece like, "Why do you think the author said that?"

We meet at 10:30, three times a week in a cinder-block seminar
room on the first floor of Dealy Hall, the same building, built in
1867, where I took my first English course in 1951. For the editors
of my new text—Robert Scholes, Nancy R. Conley, Carl H. Klaus,
and Michael Silverman—"Literature enriches our lives because it
increases our capacities for understanding and communication. It
helps us to find meaning in our world and to express it and share it
with others."

Of the 100 authors in Connolly's 1948 text, only 16 appear in
Elements of Literature. The only clearly identifiable Catholics are
Flannery O'Connor and Gerard Manley Hopkins; but there are works
by those other writers I most love to teach: Thoreau, E. B. White,
Virginia Woolf, George Orwell, James Baldwin, Joan Didion, James
Joyce, Ernest Hemingway, and Langston Hughes.

While Connolly, guided by his religious vision, designed his texts
to teach not only literature but Christian virtue to Catholic men,
these editors have collaborated to produce a marketable product which
must do three things: continue the canon—those writers like
Shakespeare, Tennyson, and Fitzgerald, without whom, presumably,
no educated person can open his mouth in public; contain enough
explanatory material to compensate for the teacher's inadequacies;
teach the new secular virtue—multiculturalism—with enough works
by blacks, women, and various minorities to satisfy a teacher who
wants to build a whole course around a political issue. The biggest
change in English teaching over thirty years, says a professor who
revered Connolly, is the imposition of political agendas on literary
texts—which agendas both distort the texts and rob the student of

the opportunity to discuss more fundamental questions about human life which the original authors pose. On the first day of class we are working with a 1500-page anthology with no up-front ideology, but 114 authors, from Sophocles to John Lennon, and we have little sense of what we and it will yield in the fourteen weeks that follow.

The 21 of us are crammed close together around narrow tables placed in a rectangle, so we have to look at each other all the time. Twelve women and eight men, four of whom have gone to Jesuit high schools. Seven are in the Business School. Two are varsity athletes—one baseball and one football. The ethnic-racial mix includes two Puerto Ricans, an Albanian, one African-American, a Ukrainian, a Nicaraguan, and the usual component of Italian and Irish. The Albanian, Lek Berishaj, resists removing his heavy leather jacket—a sign, I explain to him, that he does not intend to stay. At this point in the semester he considers himself more Albanian than American.

For about thirty years I've taught journalism, American studies, and literature at five Jesuit universities. In recent years, partly to test myself and to prove to my students that I can do what I ask them to do—write—I have traveled to international hot spots like South Africa, Syria, Iraq, Vietnam, Cuba, and Indonesia and published articles and photographs on my adventures. In Indonesia last summer I looked out the train window at miles of rice patties, lush forests, mountains and poverty-stricken farmers on the way from Jakarta to Yogyakarta and was overwhelmed by the realization of how differently God treats us all. If I had been born the son of an Indonesian rice farmer rather than of a Trenton, New Jersey, journalist, rather than know the joys of Beethoven's "Fidelio," French bread, cheese, and wine, Tolstoy, and Walden Pond, rather than teaching generations of students like those in this room, I'd be standing in a rice field in mud up to my knees, not even looking up to see this train go by.

If my personal history repeats itself, one or two of these students may take a course from me again, become my friend, running or biking partner, dinner guest and host, write to me for years, maybe even invite me to perform a wedding and baptize a child. Or bury a parent or spouse. And someone else will finish the course bitter, angry at a low grade or some other offense of which I may have been unaware.

As it happens, I must miss the second class in order to preach at a friend's wedding; so, for the long weekend, I assign nine essays, 59 pages. Two students drop the course immediately.

***

Clarilibeth Torres sits directly across from me. One day when she was twelve, looking out her South Bronx windows about thirty blocks south of Fordham, she waved to a her friend Hector on his way home from his job. He waved and smiled. Then suddenly she saw a gang of men with baseball bats beat him to the ground. They slashed his face, pounded him, ripped his shirt, and left him face-down in a pool of blood. They had stolen the gold chain Clara's mother had given Hector for his birthday. The next day she read in the paper that Hector had provoked the fight.

Now Clara, a freshman at Fordham, age twenty, is determined to master the media, write poetry, have her own web page and her own magazine. Born in Puerto Rico, she spent the first five years of her life shuttling between various aunts and grandparents in Puerto Rico and the Dominican Republic. She has never met her father, although she once called him on the phone, then hung up before he could answer. Years passed without her seeing her mother, who does not even know her birthday. Her two older brothers and three younger sisters have different fathers. When she moved to America in 1989 her mother and her mother's current boyfriend dragged her from Albany to Philadelphia to all-over Florida because "the authorities" in each town were a few steps behind the boyfriend.

Today she divides her addresses between two Bronx "aunts," commutes to lower Manhattan where she works thirty hours a week as a receptionist at Barnes and Noble, and at Fordham does her best to compete with students with more stability in their lives than she has had in hers.

At the Bayard Rustin Humanities High School in Manhattan she was a star. She won a Shakespeare recital contest, worked in an anti-drug program, joined the photo club, softball and volleyball teams, yearbook and newspaper, and edited her own magazine. The faculty loved her and encouraged her creativity; but they did not teach her intellectual discipline, spelling and grammar. Which is not necessarily their fault. Surrounded by Spanish speakers most of the day, she has settled into something she calls "Spanglish." Her favorite poet is Sylvia Plath, and she has read the Confessions of St. Augustine twice on her own; but there's an enormous gap between what's bursting out of her creative soul and what she can say in Sylvia Plath's native tongue.

When she arrived at Fordham for the HEOP (the federally funded Higher Education Opportunity Program) remedial summer courses, she loved it —a beautiful campus, students like herself. But September, when the other 3800 arrived, threw her into a funk. To her eyes, she was swamped in a sea of preppies, all cool in their J. Crew and Gap designer garb, all the middle class white people and the minorities split into their own cliques, and only the resident students in on the fun. Those high school As and Bs slipped to a 2.6. But somehow, though she is not formally religious, she believes in God's plan; she loves her courses and almost all of her teachers, and she adapts.

She fights me. When I take ten points off her quiz because she says that Robert Frost's classic poem, "Stopping by Woods on a Snowy Evening"—"Whose woods these are I think I know/ his house is in the village though"—is about "escaped slaves," because there's no evidence for that in the text, she stays after class to argue: that's her interpretation; therefore, she says, I have to give her credit.

When we do four films at the end, I assign High Noon (They have never heard of Gary Cooper!) and John Cunningham's story, "Tin Star," on which it is based; and the class unanimously prefers the story, where the sheriff—contrary to the film's lone hero who wins a shoot-out with four killers—dies, deliberately taking a bullet aimed at his deputy. But to Clara, Gary Cooper's Will Cain, the 1950s liberal's ideal man of courage, is a "coward," because he went around trying to raise a posse, rather than handle it himself.

It is the most astonishing idea I have ever heard from a student. Perhaps her imagination is so distorted by Lethal Weapon, Arnold Schwarzennegar, Sylvester Stallone, and Kung Fu movies, where comic book heroes armed with automatic weapons, and somehow never touched by the thousands of bullets that splatter earth, sand, walls, and glass around them, blow away their adversaries with machine gun bursts and flying kicks. Or rather, perhaps she reads all literature totally through the prism of her own experience. She is an escaped slave looking for a house in the snow. No posse or armed committee of townfolk have ever done anything for her, and she has survived. So Gary Cooper should quit whining and take care of himself.

***

When class goes well, it is ninety percent lively discussion; I sit with my prepared discussion outline, broken into five or ten-minute segments in front of me and a long number two pencil in my hand, look around to call on quiet people who resist getting involved, and strain with my army artillery-damaged ears to hear what to me are mumbles and whispers.

But sometimes I go to the board and outline the things I think we should have learned so far. This is important stuff, I say. And most of them sit back with their arms folded, either remembering it all or unconvinced that what I say is worth remembering. How do I look to them, talking emphatically and scrawling illegibly with my chalk? In my first semester Nonfiction Writing course, a bright sophomore, Amanda, took notes on me: "The pencil is his heartbeat: the blood of his life gushes on his student's papers in a series of X-filled circles and marks where he must have tap, tap, tapped in contemplation. The nod is the invite to enter his universe. He is the center of this universe, pulling each student onto his planet with an invisible cord that comes with the penetrating eyes that stare from behind his glasses. Sitting ramrod straight, his lean body clothed in a collared shirt and tie, he is relaxed and ready for action. If it is cold he wears a cardigan sweater, and he is reminiscent of the quintessential grandfather: strong, trusting and yet powerfully authoritative."

But I am not ready to look like a grandfather. And if I am "authoritative," why are they not all paying rapt attention? Do they not know I see their every move? Clara is doodling. Now she's talking to the boy next to her. I never reprimand in public, so I speak to her after class. To my embarrassment, she has been drawing a portrait of me. I appear as a hideous prune, with big ears, deep eyes, wrinkled, bony cheeks, bald head, and a ridged brow like those Klingons on Star Trek. She knows me well.

***

Several weeks into the course, in a rare small experiment with de-
mocracy, rather than assign my old standbys, like Thomas Gray's
"Elegy in a Country Churchyard, " I ask the class to read ahead and
pick poems they want to study. Some light on my favorites, like
Langston Hughes' "Theme for English B," about a black student at
Columbia, overlooking Harlem, who tells his instructor in a paper,
"You are white—yet a part of me, as I am a part of you." Several pick
Shakespeare's Sonnet 130, "My mistress' eyes are nothing like the
sun," in which the speaker loves his mistress, though her hair is like
wire, her cheeks are colorless, and her breath reeks. Reflecting, I think,
their own insecurity about their looks in a culture where, one tells
me, no young woman can look in the mirror and find herself thin
enough, and young men take steroids and pump iron for hours a day
to chisel their pecs and abs.

They focus too on Adrienne Rich's "Rape," in which a violated
woman graphically describes her humiliation—"the maniac's sperm
still greasing your thighs"—and implies that the policeman to whom
she must report the crime is the very man who degraded her. And
they pick Gwendolyn Brooks' "The Mother," in which a woman la-
ments, though not necessarily regrets, her several abortions. At the
end she addresses her dead children: "Believe me, I loved you all." As
Brooks has presented her, I doubt that any reader is meant to believe
her, and she may not believe herself.

***

Joseph C. DeBarbrie, tall, smooth-complexioned, gentlemanly, usually sits four seats to the left of Clara. A year before, as a senior at St.
Ignatius Prep in San Francisco, he sat in a musty, wood-paneled room
at the Jesuit retreat house outside Palo Alto, sipping Earl Grey tea
and wondering what was so great about "kairos" and "agape," the
buzz words that annually floated home from the senior retreat. Then
a retreat leader knocked, came in, and handed him an envelope bear-
ing St. Ignatius' picture and stuffed with surprise letters from family,
teachers, and friends showering him with love and praise.

Joe is the kind of boy adults find easy to praise. His family — insurance broker father and teacher mother who met at Santa Clara University and married right after graduation, his older brother and younger sister—are so happy and supportive that he sometimes sat around just enjoying them rather than studying. When surgery following a freshman year lacrosse injury to his back ended his varsity sports, he threw himself into four years of those extracurricular activities that allow the Jesuit student to thrive: manager and trainer for five teams, the yearbook and newspaper, the liturgy, cheer leader, social action, and, above all, the theater. Having been in plays and musicals—*Inherit the Wind, Our Town, Carousel*—for four years, he won the male lead in *Shadowlands* as a senior.

Not that every moment of Joe's adolescence was smooth. The over six weeks of recuperation in freshman year took him out of circulation longer than an adolescent can endure without losing out on friendships and the group. As a sophomore he drifted into the wrong bunch of friends. One night when the gang was hanging out smoking cigarettes on what they call The Avenue by the San Francisco reservoir overlooking the Pacific, his "friends" turned on him, told him bluntly that they didn't like him, and that he was out of the gang. Go home. Emotionally crushed, he staggered home in the rain.

He rebuilt himself in school activities, particularly on a school-sponsored summer "faith tour" living and working in Belfast and Dublin. In Dublin he lived at Gonzaga College and worked in a summer camp for eight to ten year-old boys strung out on dope. In Ireland, he says, the campaign against drugs resembles the American campaign against cigarettes—graphic posters of young people with rotting teeth. His little boys liked to show off the track marks between their fingers where their older brothers and pals had given them a hit. On walks he would cut through a graveyard where the boys had left their needles strewn between the tombstones.

So on retreat he relished the notes of praise; but he was most struck by the letter from his drama coach, who told him "it's time to exit stage left at the prep"; rather than applaud, his director challenged him to go on and "become a good man."

Joe picked Fordham because Jesuits "take care of their students," because he liked the pretty campus with pretty girls, because he liked the student body's economic diversity, and because he thought he "could handle New York." Though it took him a few months to be sure he had come to the right place, he soon came on strong in Residence Hall leadership, a role in the Mimes and Mummers' production of Moon over Buffalo, and a focused dedication to study that moved his high school B average to a Fordham A-. In his theology course, famed feminist theologian Elizabeth Johnson changed his image of God from the more simple, personal, someone-I-can-talk-to encounter of his high school retreat, to a God who is many things, masculine and feminine, still real, yet incomprehensible.

On Thursday nights he occasionally enjoys the local bar scene, which he sees as just one aspect of Fordham's generally healthy social milieu. True, some students party too much, but that depends on the attitude they bring with them; and better to visit the local pubs than drink on campus. Besides, he says, the neighborhood is safe. On weekends he loves to ride the "awesome" D train to Manhattan and, coming home, doesn't mind the 12 minute walk from the subway down Fordham Road.

Joe's final paper focused on three films—*Citizen Kane, Casablanca,* and *Four Feathers*—where strong men either compromise or sustain their integrity. I teach Zoltan Korda's 1939 British Empire epic, *Four Feathers,* both because it is a wonderful work of art and because its thinking and rationale, its lofty concept of duty and commitment, are so foreign to 1990s young people reluctant to commit themselves to anything beyond Saturday night's date—which they will also break if something better comes along.

***

Other things happened this semester. Tornadoes killed more than 40 persons in Oklahoma and Kansas. The Yugoslav army drove a million Albanians out of Kosovo. NATO bombings killed anywhere between 400 and 1000 innocent Serbian and Kosovar civilians by mistake. High school students gunned down their classmates. Fordham College's new dean, Jeffrey vonArx, S.J., a historian from Princeton, Yale, and Georgetown, spelled out the trustees' plan to move Fordham to greater national prominence. During Black History Month someone smeared racial and sexual insults on a door in a residence hall, prompting weeks of self-examination on the possibility of racism in our midst. Three of the five students we helped prepare for Fulbright Fellowships won. A series of Fordham Ram surveys sampling 50 students reveal that 86 percent drink and 42 percent had missed class at some time because of drinking; 88 percent could name three Shakespeare plays, but only 22 percent could name three of the 12 apostles. The Ram ran a series of articles on Ex Corde Ecclesiae, Pope John Paul II's guidelines for an authentic Catholic university; most writers seemed relatively content with Fordham's Catholic character, whatever it may be.

With the help of students and alumni who packed the gym for home games, basketball caught fire. Father Avery Dulles, S.J., who celebrated his 80th birthday and tenth year in the McGinley Chair, lectured to a crowd of 700 on "Can Philosophy be Christian?" The paper praised in its editorial the Mimes and Mummers production of Jesus Christ Superstar for casting a black Jesus and interpreting Jesus' death as his solidarity with oppressed groups everywhere—African Americans, Jews, women, and homosexuals. The Security Files report 410 incidents for the semester. These include: a Guinea pig loose in the cafeteria, a dozen stolen wallets (including mine), stolen book bags and computers, students caught with beer or marijuana, misparked cars, broken elevators, emergency illnesses, fire alarms, and two tombstones toppled in the Jesuit cemetery.

The last week of the year I visit a student friend, a senior, in the hospital. After early morning words exchanged in a local pub, he is outnumbered on the way home and beaten senseless. They have punched in his face and could have killed him. In the final month of school, we, as a nation, have been overwhelmed by the shock of American middle class boys with guns who somehow release the demons that plague them by shooting down their classmates. This madness seemed far away, in the West or South. But this beating was done not by neighborhood trouble makers, but by Fordham freshmen. My friend is victim of the alcohol culture, surely; but also of whatever it is in the American mores that says men should settle their differences with violence. We can hope that those responsible will not be back. Meanwhile, the senior, still bandaged, received his diploma in person to a standing ovation.

***

I close up my deserted sophomore dean's office a little before 5:30, trying to decide which I need more, daily mass or a quick swim. Later I'll go to the wake of a sophomore's father who has died in a fall. At a student mass in my residence hall room on Monday night we prayed for those whose lives come apart in the last weeks of class and during exams. During the semester about a half dozen have withdrawn for a while with depression. On the way to the gym I pass John, a student hospitalized two years ago, now one of our successes. His philosophy professor calls him a star; his mother says any other school would have forgotten about him.

In the campus center and Vince Lombardi Sports Complex, the newly-installed network of around-the-clock TV monitors in the lobby, cafeteria, lounge, and weight rooms has given the area the atmosphere of an airport waiting room or a sports bar without the beer. On the screen, commercials, news trivia, and MTV: performers kiss, they unbutton their clothes. After dinner I visit the Jesuit graveyard, make the rounds of the tombstones, try to decipher the names, many of which time, air pollution, and New York winters have washed away. The plan is to destroy the old stones before the elements reduce them to rubble and replace them with a little bronze plaque for each man and a statue of St. Ignatius.

It begins to rain. The skies open. The earth is drenched. Three students—two guys and a girl—cavort onto Edwards' Parade and send their Frisbee sailing through the torrent. They leap, tumble, roll, laughing, splashing in the lush green grass.

***

On the last day of class I give them a short slide show, pictures I've taken over thirty years, but mostly within the last few months. Nineteenth century Fordham: Dealy Hall, in which we sit, and Hughes Hall, in which several of us live, when they first went up. The baseball bleachers no longer on Edwards' Parade. For the group photo of the 1857 Jesuit faculty, I point out: Fr. Tissot, the Civil War chaplain; Fr. Doucet, the friend of Edgar Allan Poe; Fr. Daubresse, who taught moral philosophy but did not know English; and Fr. Legouais, the funny-looking fellow with the face of an angry goat, the dwarf, whom students loved. The Third Avenue El passing by the campus in 1916. Myself swimming in Walden Pond and sitting by Thoreau's grave. Hemingway posing with a dead leopard in Africa and kicking a can in Idaho shortly before killing himself. The campus in fall and spring.

And finally themselves. The class photo—my last class of the millennium—very few of them the same persons who sat looking at me and one another in January. Lek, though he still hates poetry and old movies, makes an exception for Four Feathers. It may help him stand up to his father who wants him to move back to Albania. The baseball player has quit the team. The football player thought of quitting, but stayed. Two of the 18 in the picture have failed the course.

Joe could go one of two ways. This summer he works for Gap in San Francisco. With a Colombian grandmother, he speaks Spanish well. Some day, as a Gap executive, he could go to Latin America and convince his company to apply Catholic social justice principles to their factories there. Or he could take some risks, take communications courses, stay in New York, "make it here," and end up host of the "Today Show."

Clara ends the year evicted by one of her aunts, split from her boyfriend, but with a solid average Fordham grade. Her favorite essay is James Thurber's short fable, "The Moth and the Star," about a young moth who ignores his parents' commands to flutter around the street lamps like the other moths and get his wings singed. Instead, every night, for years, he tries to fly to a star, as if it were right beyond the tree tops. He never reaches it, of course; but he begins to think he did, and lives a long life happy with his imagined accomplishment. His parents, brothers, and sisters all burned to death when they were young.

(Raymond A. Schroth, S.J., an assistant dean at Fordham College, is a professor of English, a journalist, a Jesuit priest, and the author of four books. He is writing a history of Fordham University—which will include the above chapter.)

Chapter Six

PILGRIM PERSON ON THE ROAD
Thomas E. Ambrogi

*Diverse religious traditions lead
to a justice spirituality*

As I look back over the journey of my life and spirit, there are several key markers along the way. I am, before all else, an ecumenical and interfaith Christian. My horizon of faith is international and multilingual. My theology has for many years been interdisciplinary, "theology and". . . politics, literature, economics. I am consumed, even sometimes obsessed, by the quest for justice: racial justice, social justice, economic justice, equality for women and for gay and lesbian people. And I am, finally, a sacramental and liturgical Christian. The most ordinary signs have the sacred capacity to effect what they signify. The world is sacrament.

I was born in 1930, of second-generation Tuscan-Irish stock. I grew up in a happy and lively family in suburban Philadelphia, the third of five children. A vital Catholic parish and parochial school nurtured me well, and I then plunged into the challenge of prep school with the Jesuits. My father died of a coronary at age 45 when I was 16, and, two years later, my mother died of cancer at age 46. I look back on those early encounters with death, somehow profoundly creative in the midst of their awful pain, as among the most formative experiences of my life.

I entered the Jesuit Novitiate at the age of 17, beginning a 15-year course of studies to ordination. During that marvelous intellectual journey, I took an M.A. in Classics at Fordham and taught Classical Languages and Literature at Georgetown University, 1954-57. Among the undergraduates who sat breathlessly at my feet during those years were Patrick J. Buchanan and Antonin J. Scalia, although I don't always admit to that in mixed company. I then went off to the University of Innsbruck for four years of theological studies, and was ordained there in the university church in 1960. Karl Rahner was then in his prime on the Innsbruck faculty, and his friendship and the excitement of his theological vision also remain among the most formative blessings of my life.

After a fifth year of spiritual and pastoral theology with the French Jesuits in the Champagne, I came home in 1962 for another year at Georgetown, this time teaching Philosophy. When I decided to do a doctoral degree in Theology, Gustav Weigel, my mentor and a Jesuit pioneer in ecumenism, convinced me to break out into what was then a new field, ecumenical theology, and my path was set toward becoming a profoundly ecumenical and interfaith Christian.

Doctoral Studies I chose the University of Strasbourg for my doctoral work because it had both a Protestant and a Catholic faculty of theology. It was in the early years of Vatican II, and my dissertation was titled Positions doctrinales de l'Église luthérienne du Synode du Missouri: Étude oecuménique. Lutherans have often chided me that an ecumenical study of Missouri must have been rather brief, but that thesis, which I immensely enjoyed doing, launched me into broad ecumenical relationships that I still cherish. I received my degree in 1965 and was called to succeed Gustav Weigel in the chair of Ecumenics at Woodstock College, the Jesuit school of theology outside Baltimore.

I served for three years as a delegate theologian for the Catholic Bishops in the national Lutheran-Catholic and the Episcopal-Catholic Conversations. In 1966, Yale Divinity School invited Woodstock College to relocate in New Haven in what would have been a precedent-setting ecumenical consortium, and I spent a year exploring that promising possibility. But the tide swung to New York when John Bennett, then President of Union Seminary, brokered an offer to bring Woodstock onto Morningside Heights in an even broader consortium with Union, Jewish Theological Seminary and Columbia University. I commuted from Woodstock to an apartment at Union for more than a year, spinning out new models of contextual theological education and negotiating library, classroom and residence space for 300 Jesuit students all over Manhattan. This exciting adventure paved the way for Woodstock to move from Maryland to Morningside Heights in 1969, but it couldn't prevent the college from closing a few years later, for many complex reasons.

During these fast-moving and challenging years, it gradually became clear that the way of celibate priesthood was no longer a growing place for me, either as Christian or as ministering person. So I resigned in peace and love from the Jesuit order in 1969, and regretted that I had no other option but to also resign what I call my "ecclesiastical" ministry. I am not an ex-priest. I am priestly person, not only by my Christian baptism, but also by the call and charism of my sacramental ordination. It has been a marvelous journey exercising that unique call to priestly ministry in many other vocational places than those involving traditional ecclesiastical roles.

My wife Donna, whom I married in the Fall of 1969, is a convert to Catholicism from the Jewish tradition, a grace which opened me to a special interfaith awareness in my theology and my spirituality. I taught for eight years in the Religious Studies Department at University of the Pacific in Stockton, California, the first Catholic to serve on that United Methodist theological faculty. I immersed myself in the new Liberation Theology which was just arriving from Latin America, and most of my courses were interdisciplinary forays bringing theology to bear on literature and the applied social sciences.

In 1976, while Donna was a law student at Stanford, we both became active members of First Presbyterian Church, Palo Alto. I was ordained a Ruling Elder there and served for three years on the Session. As I accepted those commitments, the congregation affirmed my theological conviction that it did not make sense for me to "become" a Presbyterian, that I came to membership and service in that church as a trans-denominational Christian rooted in the Catholic tradition.

Greatest Challenge My greatest challenge as ecumenical theologian and priestly person was my call to serve as Acting Dean of the Chapel at Stanford University in 1986-87, where I was both pastor of the university church and dean of religious affairs for the university. It was a wonderful year of service to the church universal in that non-denominational Christian community, and I was proud to stand in a long line of deans which includes such distinguished friends and colleagues as Davie Napier and Robert McAfee Brown. My ecumenical spirituality was also deeply enriched by my immersion in the Quaker tradition, when I later served for three years as Interim Regional Director for the American Friends Service Committee in San Francisco, Atlanta and Pasadena.

Starting with my eight years as a student in Europe, international horizons have always been an essential part of the journey and the call. A sabbatical year in the International Ecumenical Institute at Tantur, between Jerusalem and Bethlehem, brought Donna and me to Israel and the Occupied Territories just as the Yom Kippur War broke out in 1973, and that painful time has colored all my later work on Israeli-Palestinian issues. As Director of the Commission on Social Justice for the Archdiocese of San Francisco in 1980-84, I became deeply involved with U.S. foreign policy and with refugees from Central America, especially El Salvador, Nicaragua and Guatemala. In support of church workers indicted for assisting Central American refugees in the Sanctuary Movement, I set up and directed the National Sanctuary Defense Fund in 1985-86. The international focus on world hunger at Food First, the Institute for Food and Development Policy, where I was Director from 1987-90, brought me speaking and organizing engagements on food, peace and development issues in the Philippines, Japan, Taiwan and China.

My Evolving Spirituality   If you ask me to describe how my personal theology and spirituality have evolved along the stages of this pilgrimage, I now can discern several major expanding circles.

My literary and philosophical studies in seminary during the early 1950s had been heavily influenced by my fascination with the vision of a Christian Humanism that grew out of post-war French thought. When I got to Innsbruck, my earliest theology was shaped by Karl Rahner and by my admiration for his "anthropologische Theologie." That marvelous synthesis resonated well with my own personalist and existentialist philosophical instincts and it stood me in good stead during most of my years as priest and seminary professor.

And then, in my post-Jesuit activist involvements with El Salvador and Guatemala and Nicaragua, and with their refugees in our sanctuaries, I found the socio-theological synthesis of Gustavo Gutierrez and the Latin American liberation theologians more persuasive than anything to which the Spirit had so far led me. It was enormously energizing for me to discover the primary biblical image of God the Liberator, the revelation of God as the One who stands before all else on the side of the poor and the dispossessed, and who calls and empowers me to become co-creator of a world of freedom and justice and inclusive possibility.

But that primary biblical image of God the Liberator has in recent years expanded for me into the image of God the Inclusive Lover, the One who has redeemed and who has always loved all of creation into the fullness of life—including all of the sisters and all of the brothers, wherever they are across the whole human project. Our lives and our destinies are wrapped up together. In a very profound sense, none of us is free until all of us are free, and none of us is saved until all of us are saved.

I can see that a spark of that theology of Inclusive Love was planted in me back when I was Director of the Social Justice Commission in San Francisco. Urged by some ugly violence against the gay community by young Catholics in parish dance-halls, I set up a 14-member Task Force on Gay and Lesbian Issues, and asked them to write a report on what it was like to be a gay or lesbian Roman Catholic in the Archdiocese of San Francisco. They worked for a year and, with national and international coverage, we launched 10,000 copies of their 150-page report, which was in fact far more restrained and objective than I had any right to expect. However, the Task Force Report greatly disturbed my boss, Archbishop John Quinn, and I was asked for my resignation a few months later. One has only so much political capital to spend, and I've never regretted having spent some of mine on that crucially important issue.

A Place for a Pilgrim As I become more conscious of the realities of my aging and its gradual diminishments and enrichments, whole new spiritual and theological horizons of growth have opened up. In 1996, Donna and I moved from San Francisco, which we had enjoyed immensely for almost 20 years, to Pilgrim Place, an ecumenical community of retired church professionals in Claremont, California. Almost all of the markers which I can discern on the journey of my life and spirit have come to a focus in this vibrant and diverse community of elders, and growing older in such challenging company is a thoroughly energizing experience.

Pilgrim Place was begun in 1915 by the Congregational Church, and it has gradually bought up a whole tree-lined neighborhood in the town of Claremont, just off the campus of the six Claremont Colleges, and about 45 minutes east of Los Angeles. To be admitted to this community, one must come between the ages of 65 and 75, and have at least 20 years of full-time service in the church—church defined in broadly ecumenical terms, and service defined in a wide variety of careers beyond simply the ordained ministry.

There are 330 residents, representing over a dozen denominations, and many have long and fascinating histories of international service. The majority are politically and theologically progressive and many are active in a wide variety of community and church affairs. I am continually moved by the ideal of interdependence that creates a remarkable sense of community amidst this rich diversity. Most residents arrive here in their mid-sixties, as we did, so that we are in fact several generations: from the very active 60s up to many still active in their 80s and even 90s, either living independently or with some help in the Assisted Living Unit, and then to the very frail in the Skilled Nursing Center, several of whom are over 100. People really do care about, and care for, each other, and there is a commitment to support whatever is needed for each person to grow older as vitally and actively as possible.

A Way of Life The interdependence comes out in all sorts of things; it is a way of life. Unique to Pilgrim Place is that about 15% of the 330 residents receive some financial support from all the others, either to help them cover their independent living costs or to "carry them through" if their final nursing care exhausts their own resources. These funds are raised principally through a two-day Festival each November, which draws up to 10,000 people and is a major community event. There is a marvelous Arts and Crafts Center on our "campus," and through the whole year residents produce a variety of artistic creations for sale at the Festival. The whole Festival project is really a year-long, continuing event, and it keeps everyone conscious that we are an interdependent community. We never know exactly for whom we are working to raise all this money, because those names are confidential, but we do know that we are all in this together.

At noon-time dinner, the one common social event of the day, service is family-style at tables of six, according to the random determination of a computer—so that each one easily gets to know everyone else personally. There is a richness of life together—in the sharing of ideas, values, traditions and histories, and old friends and colleagues, and spiritual and artistic and musical resources, as well as in joint service projects in the broader community. In fact, a number of political and social action organizations in the neighboring community would be hard put to manage without the energy and efforts of so many Pilgrim Place residents.

All this means that I don't feel "retired" at all, just transplanted into a challenging new community of service, which is a great blessing. I have come to live into the image of Pilgrim, and whenever a bureaucratic form asks for my occupation now, instead of "retired" I simply write "pilgrim." On the road.

Another milestone has been that, in our first year here, Donna and I decided to become members of All Saints Episcopal Church in Pasadena, a large urban parish known by some as the "Riverside Church of the West." My primary faith community is at Pilgrim Place, and I have been called into whole new forms of priestly ministry here. I regularly volunteer for several months as Chaplain in the Nursing Center, where I have found myself easily recognized as priest and invited into deep pastoral and personal relationships with the sick, the dying and their families.

But All Saints is the welcome gift of a vital worshipping community, for which I have been searching after many long years in the desert. It offers theologically thoughtful preaching, excellent music, careful and imaginative liturgical action, and some 10 major social justice ministries that make a difference. For more than 20 years, it has preached and lived an articulate theology of inclusive welcome: to gays and lesbians as sisters and brothers, to women as equals, to children and youth as persons to be cared for and taken seriously just as they are. That unique inclusivity is consciously centered around the Eucharistic table. Every celebrant, while welcoming guests just before the Eucharistic Prayer, recites what has become a kind of mantra: "Whoever you are and wherever you are on your journey of faith, know that you are welcome at this table, to share in the bread and the wine made holy." The whole community means that.

So I am an active member at All Saints, and it serves as a base for my current, all-engrossing commitment to Jubilee 2000, the call for cancellation of unpayable debt in heavily indebted poor countries. It is understood by the Rector and staff that I have not become an Episcopalian, and I continue to define myself as "a trans-denominational Christian with roots in the Roman Catholic tradition." That seems to be just fine with everyone concerned, myself included.

Changed by South Africa Countless key personages and happenings have left formative traces on me along the trail of my journey. But the most formative experience of all has been, without a doubt, the two years in which Donna and I lived in South Africa, in 1993 and 1994.

As a professor at the University of Cape Town, I was asked to develop a project called "Theology and Economic Justice" which would bring together economists, theologians and community leaders to discuss values for economic planning in the new South Africa. It proved to be a wonderful vehicle for me to get to the heart of South African life in a very short time. Donna volunteered her lawyering experience with a Community Legal Resources Center in Cape Town. We came to know up close the terrible ravages of Apartheid—and hugged and listened to and cried with so many victims of what had been the most vicious system of racial oppression the world has ever known.

We also shared the terrible anxieties and the wild exhilaration of the election of Nelson Mandela and the birth of a new South Africa. Under Mandela's charismatic leadership, and now under the leadership of President Thabo Mbeki, the new South Africa is committed to a way of reconciliation and healing that is simply awesome, given the road of vengeful and violent retribution that might easily have been taken by the black majority now in power. Desmond Tutu keeps crying: "We are the Rainbow People of God. Thanks be to God!" He really means that profoundly Christian affirmation, and most South Africans have come to believe him, even as they watched him flinch in pain at the stories of torturous inhumanity that came before the Truth and Reconciliation Commission over which he presided.

One of our most moving encounters in South Africa was a long visit with Beyers Naudé, a renowned Afrikaner pastor of the Dutch Reformed Church who was defrocked by his church in 1960 when, with a ringing prophetic voice from the pulpit, he announced his powerful conviction that Apartheid was a sin. He founded the Christian Institute, which courageously led the resistance of the churches for more than a decade. He suffered an ugly ostracism from his Afrikaner peers, social and ecclesiastical, and endured long bouts of the strictest kind of banning by the South African Security Forces.

When we met Beyers, he was in his early 80s, frail and beautiful and almost translucent, with the shining eyes of a seer. I asked him what has kept him going all these years, in those times when everything seemed hopeless or in check. He replied that it was the beauty of the Black South African soul, the uncanny ability of Black South Africans to forgive, their unwillingness to call for vengeance under the lash of so much terrible suffering. And he traced this to the African value called *"Ubuntu."* In the long traditions of African tribal society, *Ubuntu* means that no one is ever fully human except in community with others. When I asked whether this was a value brought to South Africa by Christian missionaries, Beyers thought carefully and said: "No, it is an ancient, pre-Christian value deep in the African soul, a priceless gift that Africans have to teach us Christians, if only we could hear. And it is my greatest source of hope for the new South Africa."

I am a pilgrim. On the road. I read the morning papers and come away feeling that we live in a desert time. So little spice, so little verdant green, so little spark for new visions of promising wholeness in public life. But the blessed experience of our privileged time in Cape Town lives bright in my spirit. It is a sacramental beacon of hope and possibility, and the Black South African soul has taught me much about the diversity of the human family and about the inclusive love of God. *Ubuntu* is the vision: none of us is ever fully human except in community with others. None of us is saved until all of us are saved. None of us is free until all of us are free.

(*Thomas E. Ambrogi is a writer and human rights advocate, an ecumenical theologian and retired theology professor.*)

Chapter Seven

JOURNEYING

Donna Myers Ambrogi

A lawyer mines a spirituality
from her experiences

As I look back on my life, I can discern several patterns of spirituality intertwining with the major directions of my work: an abiding concern for social justice; a profound immersion in ecumenical and interfaith realities; and more recently, an orientation to aging and its unique challenges.

I was born into a Jewish family in St. Paul, Minnesota, in 1929. Political and social consciousness was a prime value in our family. While the specifically religious element of Judaism had relatively little impact on our family life, there was a strong psychological and cultural awareness of being Jewish, of being outside the dominant Catholic population in St. Paul, and definitely not welcome in certain homes, restaurants and other facilities. But most importantly, the prophetic summons to social justice in the Hebrew Scriptures was always in the forefront of my family's vision. This showed itself not only in a concern for one's own people as a minority group often discriminated against, but more fundamentally in identification with the persecuted everywhere. No one in our extended family escaped the powerful push and pull of that vision.

My social and political awareness came early in life. I recall beggars being fed in our kitchen in the Depression years. Campaigning for Franklin Roosevelt while in the second grade was the most natural thing in the world for a child whose father was the only physician in the area to display a Farmer-Labor Party bumper sticker on his car. My parents were also active in helping to rescue European Jews in the 1930's. And the deep political and social involvement of my sister, ten years my elder, gave me a sense of solidarity with the then-struggling labor unions and with the Spanish Loyalists, surely uncommon in a middle-class American child.

In 1941, my father got tired of making house calls in the Minnesota snow, and so we moved to Los Angeles. At age 16, after my junior year of high school, and just as the war ended, I entered the University of Chicago. This was in the exciting era of the Hutchins Great Books program, and it was an intellectual experience from which I have never recovered. My extra-curricular activities were those you might expect of someone with my background: ringing doorbells to campaign for a Socialist professor running for Congress, helping a slum-area family paint their home, lobbying in Washington against universal military training, picketing department stores which refused to hire black salespeople. My burning passion, however, was the labor movement, and in my summer jobs and my studies in the Social Sciences I moved toward a career in the field of workers' education.

Changing Direction   But another force intervened and propelled me onto a deep religious journey which took me in a different direction. The University of Chicago was a place of intense intellectual and spiritual search for me, as for so many others in those days. A thirst for truth, for answers to ultimate questions about the meaning of life was far more important than the pursuit of a degree as an economic passport. At the University, I was no longer part of a beleaguered minority. Now I could calmly answer the usual questions about religious affiliation, "Yes, I was born Jewish, but it is not my religion." A persistent sense of God led me to search in what was, during that era at the University, the socially and intellectually unacceptable realm of religion.

I was never drawn to involvement in the Hillel Foundation, and my studies, liberal though they were, failed to expose me to the best of Jewish thought. Instead, I encountered Quaker pacifists, Unitarian seminarians, and finally, a remarkable group of Catholic graduate students, called "The Community" by those who knew them. Their keen minds and deeply Christian outlook, embracing the intellectual life of the campus and the social needs of the world around them, provided for me a sense of "homecoming" within the atmosphere of search which characterized the University. Through them I was exposed to vital experiences of the liturgy and to the best of post-war French Catholic thought, from de Lubac and Cardinal Suhard to the priest-workers and Jocist Catholic Action.

During my sixth and last year at the University, after considerable soul-searching, I was baptized in the Catholic Church. After completing my M.A. in Social Sciences, I worked for the Catholic Labor Alliance in Chicago, which enlarged my understanding of the Church's social teachings.

Taking a Chance Through a chance meeting with Professor Yves Simon and his wife, I was told about the Grail, a dynamic international Catholic laywomen's movement. In 1952, I went for a time of "apostolic formation" to Grailville, national center of the Grail, located in Loveland, Ohio. Their remarkable approach to Christian deepening—integrating body, mind and spirit, theology, liturgy and culture—opened up for me new vistas of spiritual growth that were really earth-shaking. Living within this diverse community of women, I had the opportunity to develop all sorts of ways to be myself. For the next 17 years, I worked full-time in the Grail. I founded a religious book and art shop in Philadelphia, worked with international students in New York City's International House, lectured and wrote on a variety of subjects, and directed adult education programs.

The role of women in church and society was one direction in which I was naturally propelled in my Grail work and study. Today I blush to recall the 90-minute talks I gave to numerous groups on the "complementarity of men and women." Nonetheless, the Grail's vision of women's potential, and the need to liberate this potential from the temporal and spiritual bondage in which most women exist, was a powerful force in my life. This vision fed me well in my later work with Equal Rights Advocates, the Older Women's League, and a women's human rights organization in South Africa.

Almost from the beginning of my life in the Grail, my heart was captured by the budding possibilities of ecumenism. On a Fulbright grant in 1957, studying adult education in the Netherlands, I participated in my first ecumenical conferences long before there was significant dialogue between Catholics and Protestants elsewhere. When I returned to the United States, I helped the Grail develop contacts with Protestant theologians and local church members, at a time when Catholic priests were not yet permitted to engage in such dialogue. For several years in the 1960's, I edited Ecumenical Notes, an exploratory little journal which had a considerable list of national and even international subscribers.

As a Catholic observer, I participated in the 1963 conference of the World Student Christian Federation in Athens, Ohio, and wrote a meditation for the conference prayer booklet. A high point for me was participation as a journalist in the 1963 World Faith and Order Conference in Montreal. I also helped develop local ecumenical discussion-action groups at several Grail centers, worked with a World Council of Churches project to establish a national ecumenical women's dialogue group, and served on the U.S. Catholic Bishops' Committee on Education for Ecumenism. Packard Manse, a Protestant conference center in Stoughton, Massachusetts, invited me to become its first Catholic staff member. This led me to meetings with Protestant and Catholic clergy and laity throughout New England, as well as to two nights as the sole woman in a Williamston, North Carolina jail, as part of an SCLC group attempting to desegregate public eating facilities in 1964.

Back to School   These diverse experiences made me aware of my need for further theological education, and so I embarked on graduate studies in theology at the University of San Francisco and the Graduate Theological Union in Berkeley, receiving an M.A. in 1970. In conjunction with this, I spent a semester at the Ecumenical Institute in Bossey, Switzerland, where the daily consciousness of our Christian divisions at the celebration of the Eucharist proved increasingly painful to me. I also served as a WCC intern at Scottish Churches

House in Dunblane, Scotland, again as the first Roman Catholic staff member.

Soon after, I was appointed director of fieldwork at the Jesuit School of Theology in Los Gatos, California. I was the first woman on their faculty, and found being "token woman" a more daunting experience than either Packard Manse or Dunblane, where I had been the first Catholic. I then joined the ecumenical campus ministry team at Stanford, during the early tumultuous years of U.S. involvement in Vietnam. As an intentional ecumenical act I shared a house in Palo Alto with Barbara Troxell, a Methodist minister also on the campus ministry staff. I thereby acquired a new "sister" who broadened my vision considerably, and in 1969 we helped propel the Grail to expand its membership to include Protestants. It was during this time, in the course of our common ecumenical concerns, that I first met Gene Bianchi.

I met my future husband in 1966 at a post-Vatican II ecumenical conference at the University of Notre Dame. Tom Ambrogi and I were married three years later at First Presbyterian Church in Palo Alto, with my Methodist housemate Barbara officiating. In the early years of our marriage, Tom and I lived in Stockton, California, where I worked as a Community Health Planner and taught Consumer Health Education at a local community college.

At age 44, feeling myself to be too much a generalist in many directions, I decided to become a lawyer as a centering point for my commitments to social change. I took the LSAT exam the day before Tom and I left for a five-month sabbatical in the Middle East. After a remarkable month in Lebanon, Jordan and Egypt, we arrived at the Ecumenical Institute at Tantur, on the edge of Jerusalem, just ten days before the 1973 Yom Kippur War erupted. That time in Israel and the West Bank was one of the most challenging experiences of my life, as I attempted to understand more profoundly my Jewish-Christian identity in the midst of a conflict of seemingly irreconcilable opposites.

At Stanford Law School I was by ten years the eldest student in my year, and so, for the first time I began to develop a consciousness of aging issues. I volunteered with a Legal Services program for elders, and worked with a public interest law firm dealing with sex discrimination issues. After becoming an attorney at age 48, I worked with the National Labor Relations Board and the U.S. Department of Labor in San Francisco, and helped in the founding of the Older Women's League.

Invitation I Couldn't Refuse It took me all of ten minutes to respond to an invitation to leave employment in the federal government and to found a statewide legal support center assisting advocates of the frail elderly, called California Law Center on Long Term Care. For the next ten years I wrote legislation, lobbied in Sacramento, did legal research and writing, trained advocates and elders, and helped organize on the whole range of issues in long term care and patients' rights. I have also taught Aging Law and Health Law and Ethics, at U.C. Berkeley and a number of other universities, and have served on several medical ethics committees in local hospitals and retirement facilities.

All of this has made my plunge into the law very worthwhile. It was indeed a creative way to pursue my commitment to meaningful social justice work, and it has unquestionably led me to a deeper understanding of the legal, economic and social-psychological issues of aging. And again I encountered Gene Bianchi, as he began his pioneering research into the spirituality of elders.

In 1993, Tom and I went to South Africa for two years of volunteer work, and this was the most formative of all the social justice challenges of my life. In Cape Town I worked with the Legal Resources Center and with Black Sash, the national women's human rights group. In 1994 Tom and I were fortunate to be asked to train observers for the first democratic election in South Africa's history, and we ourselves served as observers in that momentous event. We left a good part of our hearts in South Africa, and are profoundly grateful that, five years later, we were able to return for a wonderful visit there.

In 1996 we moved to Pilgrim Place, the ecumenical community of retired church professionals in Claremont, California, which Tom describes at some length in the account of his journey. I will say only that it is an altogether remarkable place to live out the adventure of the last third of my life. It is surely not a place in which to "retire." Rather, it constantly challenges me to reach out more imaginatively to share with others, in their (and in my own) moments of need. At the same time it calls me to go to an ever deeper level of inner awareness.

Now no longer bound to the strictures of full-time employment, I am profoundly grateful for the luxury of time, although our days in this community are so full that it is still a struggle to find space for reading and for meditation. I am chair of Pilgrim Place's Health and Welfare Committee, serve on a hospital ethics committee, and work every week at a community food bank. I also teach occasionally at a nearby university and continue my involvement in the Grail and in a statewide advocacy organization for nursing home reform.

I am daily moved by the vital 90-year olds at Pilgrim Place, and by the indomitable spirit of so many residents caring for increasingly frail loved ones. Death and dying are ever-present realities in this community of elders, challenging me to come to terms with growing diminishment in my own life, even as I share in others' struggles to live as fully as possible to the end. A recent bout with breast cancer has made me more deeply aware of how important it is to me to live in a caring community. I am convinced that the tangible and spiritual support which I have received from fellow residents has helped significantly in my recovery.

Like Tom, I have moved beyond my once vital and extremely meaningful participation in the Roman Catholic Church, to a new, more ecumenical and inclusive place. Contact with so many faithful and searching Protestant Christians at Pilgrim Place continually challenges my own understanding and faith. This experience, together with weekly liturgies at All Saints Episcopal Church in Pasadena, where we are committed members, draws me deeper into my ongoing spiritual journey, and keeps me ever more attuned to the cries of the world beyond.

From a Jewish home to the Grail to Pilgrim Place. Journeying— the personal and communal search for unfolding mystery—is the metaphor of choice.

(*Donna Myers Ambrogi, an attorney and university professor, has been active her whole life in social justice concerns and legislation. She and her husband, Thomas, live at Pilgrim Place in Claremont, California.*)

Intermezzo II

To be a self is
to own a story. . .

The self at any given moment is a made self—it is not a solid independent machine for deciding and acting efficiently or rationally in response to stimuli, but is itself a process, fluid and elusive, whose present range of possible responses is part of a developing story. The self is—one might say—what the past is doing now. It is continuity and so it is necessarily memory—continuity seen as the shape of a unique story, my story, which I own, acknowledge as mine. To be a self is to own such a story: to act as a self is to act out of the awareness of this resource of a particular past.

Rowan Williams in *Resurrection*

Chapter Eight

A SPIRITUALITY CATHOLIC
AND COMMUNITARIAN
Charles E. Curran

Through controversy a scholar refines
the core of his religious view

To put on paper how my theological work has affected my spirituality—in honoring my colleague Eugene Bianchi—is a welcome challenge. Gene has contributed a lot to theology and religious studies over the years. I first met him at a post-Vatican II conference in 1966 and have been in contact with him ever since. At his instigation I contributed an essay to an earlier volume edited by himself and Rosemary Ruether on democracy in the church.

The topic fits very well into my own discipline of moral theology or Christian ethics. It stresses the person, the self. The danger in much of moral theology comes from giving primary importance to external acts rather than to the person. Acts or what we do are important, but the person is even more fundamental in moral theology. The person is both subject and agent. A biblical metaphor reminds us that the good tree brings forth good fruit while the bad tree brings forth bad fruit. From the good tree (person) comes good fruit (acts). My actions both express who I am but also help to shape me as a subject and person.

Shaping My *Self* Most often we go about our daily life without thinking about how our work and actions both express and shape ourselves as persons. This essay accords me the opportunity to consciously and explicitly reflect on how my work in theology has both expressed but also shaped my own self and my spirituality. In the process of writing, I have come to recognize the importance of a catholic and communitarian spirituality that understands my relationship to God not simply as an individual relationship with a loving mother and father but as a relationship to a community of the people of God, and in fact ultimately to all humanity and the created earth itself.

How did I arrive at this understanding and approach? I have spent my academic life teaching, researching, and writing in the area of Catholic moral theology and Christian ethics. I received two doctorates in Rome in 1961 (before the Second Vatican Council) but was heavily influenced by the new approach to moral theology proposed by Bernard Haring and Joseph Fuchs. Thus, from the very beginning I was opposed to the minimalistic, legalistic, and act-centered morality of the school manuals of moral theology and argued for a broader biblical, liturgical, personal, growth-oriented morality. This vision has remained constant in my work for forty years, but I could not have dreamed forty years ago where my work in moral theology would take me.

For instance, in the 1960s I began to question the Catholic teaching on artificial contraception and masturbation and argued for the legitimacy of theoretical and practical dissent within the church on these issues. Later in the 60s and 70s I realized that many of the methodological and ecclesiological problems involved in the absolute prohibition of artificial contraception for spouses were also present in other specific moral questions. Thus, I had to argue for the justification of dissent in a number of specific areas such as sterilization, artificial insemination, divorce, homosexuality, the beginning of human life, and the solution of conflict situations by the principle of double effect. Ironically I continued to insist that moral theology involves more than the consideration of individual moral acts, but for someone writing in the Catholic tradition at that time these particular acts became very significant issues.

These positions and related actions on my part had significant repercussions for my life in the Catholic Church. As a priest of the diocese of Rochester, New York, I began teaching moral theology in St. Bernard's Seminary in Rochester in 1961, but by 1965 the diocesan authorities told me I could no longer teach in the Seminary because of my views. However, with their blessing I went to the Catholic University of America in 1965. But in 1967 the trustees of Catholic University voted not to renew my contract because of my positions on some of the sexual issues. When that news got out, a university-wide strike by fellow faculty and students closed down the university and convinced the trustees to change their mind. This much publicized incident at Catholic University thrust me into a leadership position in moral theology despite my young age. And this was formative of my sense of myself.

Turning Point In 1968 Pope Paul VI issued his encyclical Humanae vitae condemning artificial contraception. As it turned out, I was the leader and spokesperson for a group of theologians at Catholic University who just one day after the encyclical was published issued a statement ultimately signed by over 600 Catholic academicians maintaining that one could in theory and in practice disagree with the conclusion of the papal teaching and still be a loyal Roman Catholic. At that point the trustees at Catholic University set up an academic inquiry to see if we theologians had violated our academic responsibilities as Catholic theologians at Catholic University. In the end the faculty committee and the Academic Senate of the University exonerated us. However, my positions in these matters coupled with my professorship at Catholic University continued to occasion controversy and strong disagreement from more conservative sectors in the Catholic Church.

Then, in 1979 the Congregation for the Doctrine of the Faith informed me that they were investigating my moral theology. After a seven-year investigation by mail and a very challenging personal questioning in Rome, the Congregation for the Doctrine of the Faith with the approval of the Pope concluded that I was no longer suitable nor eligible to be a professor of moral theology. On the basis of that decision the trustees at Catholic University of America decided that I could no longer teach Catholic theology there. As a result of the Vatican action no Catholic institution would offer me a full-time tenured teaching position. However, I have found a very hospitable and challenging academic home at Southern Methodist University. And again, this had an impact on my spirituality and my deepest sense of myself.

Since then, in my judgment the Roman Catholic Church under the restorationist pontificate of Pope John Paul II has become even more authoritarian and control conscious. Not only has the church refused to change on any of the issues that have been under discussion but it has issued very authoritarian and defensive documents, continued to use in its moral theology one particular philosophical approach, and appointed very conservative bishops throughout the world. Women in the Catholic Church have especially felt their second-class citizenship. Very recently my friends Jeannine Gramick and Robert Nugent have been prohibited from exercising their very supportive ministry to gays and lesbians and their parents. Yes, over-all there are some very positive aspects in the life of the Catholic Church today but the negative aspects have become very oppressive. Despite my own personal hurt at what has happened to me and others, I have decided to stay in the church and work for its reform despite all the problems. A catholic spirituality lies behind this decision.

Catholic Spirituality, Pilgrim Church By a catholic (small c) spirituality I mean a spirituality that recognizes that one belongs to an ecclesial community which strives to be universal and all-embracing. A catholic spirituality is not necessarily limited only to the Roman Catholic Church and in fact a catholic theological and spiritual understanding can rightly criticize some contemporary aspects of Roman Catholicism. This five-point section will develop my approach to a catholic spirituality from the viewpoint of one slightly battered Roman Catholic theologian.

1. **The Catholic understanding of the church** well illustrates the Catholic insistence on mediation—the divine is mediated in and through the human as illustrated above all in the Incarnation: the divine becoming human in Jesus of Nazareth. I have clung to this conviction. The church as the human community of the disciples of Jesus with human leadership and office holders mediates the risen Jesus through the power and presence of the Spirit. Such an under-

standing involves a magnificent and positive statement about the human. A major problem in the Catholic tradition has been the danger of too closely identifying the human with the divine and forgetting about the pilgrim nature and even sinful nature of the church. Yes, the divine is mediated in and through the human, but the human never perfectly mirrors the divine. I must accept that fact.

2. **The church is, to my mind, not a voluntary society** but God's way of being present to us. In this country we stress the voluntary nature of many societies. We join a group or a society to help ourselves as individuals to achieve our goals with like-minded people. But reflect that the family as the basic human community is not a voluntary society. The Judeo-Christian tradition insists that God made a covenant with a People and did not primarily choose, or covenant with, any individual. God's saving love comes to us in and through this community of the whole People of God. I do not join the church or stay in the church because I choose it as the best way to nurture my spiritual life. I belong to the church because as a Catholic I see it as the way God, in Christ, and through the Spirit, has chosen to be present to God's People. Such an understanding also explains why people like myself will struggle to reform and change the church even if they disagree with some aspects of it.

3. **The church strives to be an all-embracing community** overcoming the divisions of language, race, nationality, and culture. There is neither Jew nor Greek, male nor female. Such an all-embracing community calls for a spirituality that is willing to overcome the barriers that so often divide people. The challenge in such an inclusive community involves holding together the legitimate needs for both unity and diversity.

Without doubt the Roman Catholic Church has often failed to live out this most important aspect of its own catholicity. Too often Roman Catholicism substituted uniformity for unity. Today we are much more conscious of the great diversity in our world and in our church. The challenge is to preserve unity in the midst of such legitimate and necessary pluralism and diversity. The basic criteria to attain such diversity and unity comes from the ancient church axiom—in necessary things, unity; in doubtful things, freedom; in all things, charity.

Unity involves those aspects that are core to the Catholic faith. The core realities have to be accepted by all precisely because they give the church community its basic identity—the Trinity, Jesus Christ as Redeemer, the continuing work of the Holy Spirit, the forgiveness of sin, the role of the church, the sacramental system, a role for bishops and the bishop of Rome, and basic truths found in the Creed.

The contemporary Roman Catholic Church has too often forgotten the distinction between what is core to faith and what is more removed and remote. Obviously not all aspects of church teaching are core and central. However, even here pre-Vatican II theology appreciated this distinction. Such a theology recognized "theological notes" which were attempts to discern how core and central a certain teaching is. The well-known distinction between noninfallible and infallible teaching tends in the same direction. However, the Vatican, at the present time, has often been unwilling to recognize the importance of this distinction between what is core and what is remote and has even been claiming core status for some aspects that cannot be core such as moral teachings on abortion or homosexuality.

A truly Catholic understanding of unity and diversity argues strongly against the overly centralized understanding of the church as found in canon law and in the present structures of Roman Catholicism. However, the Roman Catholic tradition itself has a better approach for a more adequate structuring of the church—the principle of subsidiarity. In Catholic social teaching the state is basically good and necessary but also limited. The state is only one aspect in the totality of human civil society. The principle of subsidiarity, coming from the Latin word for "help," serves as a criterion for determining the proper role of the state.

"Subsidiarity" requires explanation.

Human society begins with the individual person, then the family, other given associations such as neighborhoods, a myriad number of voluntary associations such as professional groups, labor unions, colleges and universities, the press, the arts, and finally all the different levels of government beginning with the local through the state and finally the federal. The principle of subsidiarity maintains that the higher units should do all they can to help the more basic units to achieve their own purposes and should themselves only do those things that cannot be accomplished by the more basic units. Think, for example, of the problem of housing. Government itself encourages individuals to achieve their own housing by providing tax breaks for those who have mortgages. Government at all levels should also help voluntary associations such as Habitat for Humanity to provide housing for people. But the problems associated with providing adequate housing for all citizens are so great that individuals, families, and intermediate institutions alone cannot solve the problem, and the government itself must step in to what all the others cannot do.

The principle of subsidiarity applied to the church argues strongly against the overly centralized structure existing at the present time. More importance must be given in church structures to national and local churches and to all the people of God. Such changes do not deny the need for petrine and episcopal offices in the church but recognize the role of the local churches in accord with the accepted concepts of collegiality and the *sensus fidelium* (the sense of the faithful).

Every community including the Catholic Church will always need authority. Without authority there can be no true community of any kind. However, a great difference exists between authority and authoritarianism. At its best the Roman Catholic tradition has a good understanding of authority in theory, but the practice has not always lived up to the theory. In the Christian tradition, what is the basic virtue the community asks for its rulers? The answer: wisdom, not power. The person in charge needs the wisdom to know what is good for the community and thus to be able to bring about the common good. The prototype of such a gift is the wisdom of Solomon. Thomas Aquinas proposed a similar understanding of authority with regard to morality. Aquinas asked the question: Is something commanded because it is good or is it good because it is commanded? Aquinas strongly insists on the first—something is commanded because it is good. The will of authority does not make something good or bad. Authority must conform itself to the true and the good. Aquinas insists on the rational aspect of authority and not the voluntarist. The will does not make something good or bad. For the same reason Aquinas willingly accepted the need for civil disobedience.

Such a concept of authority opposes the very notion of authoritarianism.

4. Membership in the Church Catholic, therefore, calls for a catholic spirituality that gives a primary importance to the community. Single-issue politics destroys the civil community and does the same for the ecclesial community. Churches of all types and denominations are constantly divided over various issues. Today the issue of homosexuality has come to the fore in many Christian churches. In the Roman Catholic Church, in addition to these other issues, the issue of the role of women in ministry remains very troublesome. A catholic spirituality is willing to struggle for what seems to be true and good on noncore issues even if the total church of the present time does not accept it. However, this does not mean that one gives up working for such change. Long ago St. Paul said that he would abstain from eating the meat sacrificed to the idols, even though there was nothing wrong with it, if this became a problem for other members of the church community.

One's commitment to the church community must be stronger than one's commitment to a particular issue. I can appreciate how some women have decided to leave the Roman Catholic Church because of the oppressive structure they feel, but I also admire and support those women who stay in the church and try to change it.

The catholicity and universality of the church stand as a challenge to the particularism and limitations that can affect all of us as persons, as members of a particular profession, race, culture, or language group. A Catholic spirituality protests against any absolutization of what is only finite and partial.

A Catholic spirituality differs from a congregational approach. The Catholic approach integrates the congregation within a universal and all-embracing community so that the individual congregation cannot be absolutized. Congregations have to work together with other congregations within the inclusive body of the church in an attempt to arrive at what is best for the church.

5. The church is a pilgrim church. The Church Catholic is on a journey toward the new heaven and the new earth. Eschatology reminds us that the church will always be imperfect and also sinful. The church never fully lives up to the gospel challenge.

Roman Catholicism has recognized the eschatological and pilgrim nature of the church at Vatican II but a poor understanding of the church's role has too often identified the church as pure, holy, and without spot. The Holy Spirit is present in the church community but the church always falls short of what it should be. The sinful church is constantly in need of change and reform. Church members recognize the need to work to overcome the sinfulness of the church, but we must also be careful to remember our own sinfulness and avoid the danger of self-righteousness. The Church Catholic calls for a spirituality of action trying to work for change but also recognizes the church like all its members will never be perfect.

The tension created by living in a pilgrim church will never disappear. Christians are often tempted to think that there might have been a time when these tensions and differences did not exist among the community of the disciples of Jesus. However, even the early Christian community in the first century suffered from the tensions of a pilgrim church. In practically every letter, Paul points out the problems and abuses that are now taking place in the local church to which he is writing. Recall that Paul at Antioch withstood Peter to his face. We are told that John the Evangelist changed the Synoptics' emphasis on love of enemies to love of the sisters and brothers in the community precisely because of the disarray existing in the churches he was writing for.

Congenial Atmosphere Therefore despite my strong disagreements with some noncore aspects of contemporary Roman Catholicism, I find the Catholic theological tradition in general to be very congenial. In particular Catholic social ethics presents a compelling picture of human life in this world. In the mid 1970s I made a conscious decision to spend more time and energy on Catholic social ethics. Before that time I had concentrated on sexual and medical ethics, but I began to realize that many other Catholic theologians were dealing with sexual and medical ethics but that social ethics was being neglected. However, I also continued to keep up my work on issues in fundamental moral theology.

Catholic social ethics strongly recognizes the communal aspects of human existence. The Scriptural description of creation reminds us that all human beings are brothers and sisters who are children of the one God whom we call mother and father. The Scriptures also insist that God formed a community with a people and did not primarily deal with people as individuals. The twofold commandment of love of God and love of neighbor reminds us that our relationship to God can never be seen apart from our relationship to others. In the Catholic tradition Thomas Aquinas took over the Aristotelian notion that human beings are by nature social and political. Thus we are called by God and by our very being to live in social and political communities and not as isolated individuals.

Such an anthropology with its insistence on the human being as both sacred and social undergirds the Catholic understanding of human society. The origin of political society does not come from the need of isolated individuals to come together to arrange what is best for the individual who needs to coexist with other individuals. Human political society is instead something natural and necessary for the human person and therefore ultimately good even though it must be limited by the principle of subsidiarity as mentioned above. The purpose of the human political society or the state involves not just the good of individuals or the good of the collectivity as a whole but the common good, the good of the total community that ultimately redounds to the good of the individual member. Such a position rejects individualism that so stresses the individual that it forgets about the community and collectivism that so stresses the collectivity that it forgets about the individual.

On the basis of this communal anthropology, Catholic social ethics emphasizes not only commutative justice that exists between two individuals but also distributive and social or contributive justice. Distributive justice governs the relationship between society and individuals and unlike commutative justice is not blind and involves proportional and not arithmetic equality. Thus, in distributing the burdens of taxation within society those who have more should pay a greater percentage of their wealth in taxes. A Christian communitarian anthropology recognizes that God created the world to serve the needs of all human beings and puts significant limits on private property in the light of this universal destiny of the goods of creation to serve the needs of all. In such an approach every human being has the right to a minimally decent human existence and society has an obligation to provide for such a basic minimum. Moreover, a Christian communitarian view of society stresses the preferential option for the poor. Such an approach also recognizes the need not only for political rights (freedom of religion, speech, association, press, etc.) but also social and economic rights such as the right to food, clothing, shelter, education, and health care.

Individualism constitutes the greatest opposition to communitarianism. Unfortunately, especially in the United States, individualism is at times rampant. Many people are interested only in themselves and do not care about others. They believe that the best government is the least government. In the midst of all our diversity and differences, can the U.S. as a nation ever claim to be "we the people?" Our cities are terribly divided between and among races and economic groups. The gaps and the differences are ever widening between the haves and the have nots in our society. Ecological problems remind us of the terrible consequences of individualism. Centrifugal forces are rampant in every part of the world. Individualism and tribalism often come to the fore. We exist in a global relationship—but without a global anthropology and spirituality as well as global institutions, we will not be able to restrain the dominating economic forces that are now so active in our world. The need for this communitarian and global spirituality has never been more pressing. One must strive to work for inclusive and all-embracing communities on every level even though the larger the community, the harder this will be to achieve.

A New Spirituality Thus my work in social ethics has brought me to the realization that life in the world calls for a communitarian spirituality. This is comparable to the catholic spirituality necessary for life in the Church Catholic. However, the two settings I find myself in—of world and church—are obviously not totally separated. The challenge is the same in both—to form a community that respects diversity and differences but still holds on to unity and ultimately tries to promote the common good of all. The challenge for both is difficult; but from my perspective if the church cannot succeed, the world community will never succeed.

Of the two, the church has many more factors going for it in its attempt to achieve a true community—the presence of the risen Lord and the grace of the Spirit, the call to forgiveness and love of enemies, an understanding of love that is all-embracing, and a special concern for the poor and the needy. If the church cannot achieve some success in forming an all-embracing community there seems to be little hope for the wider community.

Thus the challenge to the church comes not only from its own internal catholic dynamic but also from the needs of the broader society to demonstrate the possibility of creating an all- inclusive community in the midst of all the differences and diversities of our time. And each member may hope to develop a personal spirituality and sense of selfhood that encompasses, however inadequately, all the main dimensions of social ideals both worldwide and communitarian.

(*Charles E. Curran, a foremost authority in the field of Moral Theology, is the author of many books, and is Elizabeth Scurlock University Professor of Human Values at Southern Methodist University.*)

Chapter Nine

PROVIDENCE WORE
A JESUIT CASSOCK

Robert Blair Kaiser

*Journalism continues a
religious vocation*

I met my first Jesuits when I was in the 8th grade, and, under their influence, became a precocious convert to Catholicism at age 13. Before then, I'd aspired to West Point. Now I shifted gears, hoping I had the right stuff for the Jesuits, whom I saw as elite soldiers of Christ, serving as they did in far flung missions from Alaska to Arabia, or teaching in high powered prep schools, or holding forth in college classrooms, or achieving eminence as scholars and scientists and theologians. Some German Jesuits, I was told, were drafting encyclicals for Pope Pius XII himself.

Naturally, I endowed the Jesuits with all the qualities of Mountbatten's commandos and Hoover's FBI, and it was no big sacrifice when, I entered the California Province of the Society of Jesus on August 15, 1948. Eugene C. Bianchi entered on the same day. We were both 17, and we spent almost ten years together, took our simple vows together at the Novitiate of the Sacred Heart in Los Gatos, studied classical languages (Laughing and Grief) in what we called the Juniorate, and then Aristotelian philosophy at Mt. St. Michael's in Spokane, Washington. We taught together in the period known as

Regency at St. Ignatius High School in San Francisco, Jesuits-in-training who worked 18-hour-days, teaching English and Latin and running Sodalities and correcting papers and coaching the kids. I coached JV football. Gene coached the debaters.

And then, toward the end of Regency, I left the Society, not because I didn't want to keep answering the Call of the Kingdom, as I had earnestly promised and I'd do every time I made the Exercises, but rather because I *did* -- and found that I couldn't answer the call any longer under superiors who didn't want me to do the job I'd been assigned. And if I couldn't do the job, then the sacrifices demanded by the three vows were no longer worth it.

Obedience First   One example (among many): I was the moderator, or publisher, of the school magazine, Inside S.I., a pretty good imitation of Time that often seemed to demand my guiding presence down at the high school until 2 a.m. At that hour, I had to climb up the fire escape to get back in the faculty residence, then, lazy lout, sleep in until 6 a.m. (instead of the mandated 5 o'clock reveille). "You're not a good Jesuit," I was told by the Father Minister. When I explained about my work down at the high school, he said that God didn't need my work. More important to go to bed at 10 and get up at 5.

Uh huh, I thought, God doesn't need my work. But the kids do. So I went on being a bad Jesuit, and tried to imagine how I could hang in there as a bad Jesuit for the rest of my days. The younger, most zealous Jesuit priests in the community seemed to be bad Jesuits, too, in the eyes of the men they called horses asses who, paradoxically, were in the saddle. "It's a metaphysical problem," the young fathers agreed. "How can there be more horses asses than horses in the Society? And how is it that all the horses asses are in the saddle?" Underneath the laughter, however, they were becoming bitter, and I could imagine myself looking a lot like them in ten years or so. So, in December 1957, I signed papers to leave the Society. But I remained, and remain, a Jesuit at heart -- an identity that has given meaning to my life and my work.

I might have stayed a Jesuit if I'd entered ten years later, because in the years after Vatican II, the Society under Father General Pedro Arrupe, like the Church itself, had become more human, and more humane. After the Council, for example, Jesuit scholastics didn't have to get up at five goddamn o'clock in the morning, not if they had to work until two. But in 1957 the men who ran the California Province, at least, were still operating under the Roothaan Principle: if it gives pleasure, avoid it, if it gives pain, embrace it.

Jan-Philip Roothaan was the General of the Society from 1829 to1853, in a fear-ridden Society of Jesus that had pulled in its horns after its suppression by the Vatican in 1773. He helped mold nineteenth century Jesuits according to a very stern model. Early twentieth century Jesuits, following the same model, never seemed to know how much freedom was at the heart of its early and most authentic tradition.

In 1997, Loyola University Press came out with a startling book by the Oregon Jesuit, Joseph Conwell, *Impelling Spirit,* that recounted Conwell's discovery in the Jesuit archives in Rome of an old, forgotten paradigm for the Society of Jesus, a new model for the future Society in a seminal document, written a year before Pope Paul III first approved the Society in 1540. St. Ignatius and his original nine companions wrote this charter for the signature of Pope Paul III. Then it was laid aside and lost in the archives for centuries. That document, said Conwell, has to erase our old view of Ignatius as the soldier-saint, a man of steely will, a coldly rational, orderly administrator. Conwell says that was an old, false portrait, one that actually "betrayed Ignatius and his first companions and has long pervaded both the practical application of the Spiritual Exercises and the practical living out of the Constitutions of the Society of Jesus."

Conwell's new view gives the rationale for an impelling spirit that had, somehow despite Roothan, characterized the pioneering Jesuits I have known. "That impelling spirit," according to Conwell, "is the Holy Spirit, passionate, creative, innovative, wildly beyond the rational, propelling, driving, pushing, blowing like an untamed hurricane with no predictable path."

Why I Left   I like to think that I was impelled by that same Spirit when I checked out of the Society's official ranks. I did so, not because I no longer wanted to "Christify the universe" (a romantic, Teilhardian formulation) but because I did. And I ended up daring greater things than I could have dreamed of doing had I stayed in the long black line.

I was still a Jesuit at heart when I moved into a journalism career. I did so with ease. I had done my M.A. thesis on journalism ethics, so I already had a pretty firm fix on journalism's reason for being, and the Jesuits had taught me how to write, so all I needed was a little practice. The first story I ever did for *The Arizona Republic* won me an Arizona Press Club award for the best feature story of the year. During my three years at *The Republic*, I won all kinds of other awards. My publisher even put me in for a Pulitzer Prize, for an 8-part series on the Navajos. And when I was sent out to the home of the Henry and Clare Booth Luce in May of 1961 to interview one of their house guests, I saw the hand of Providence at work. (For me, Providence often wore a Jesuit cassock.)

The house guest turned out to be Martin D'Arcy, English Assistant to the Jesuit General, and author of *The Mind and Heart of Love*, a difficult work, but not too difficult for me to engage the great Father D'Arcy in a conversation about it that impressed the hell out of Clare Booth Luce. She sat in on the interview, open-mouthed, and wondered afterward what I wanted to do with my life. I took a deep breath and said I thought I wanted to work for *Time*. Preparations were then under way for the Second Vatican Ecumenical Council, and I had already told the Associated Press and the United Press that I wanted to cover it. Now, it seemed, it was possible that I could overvault the wire services and go straight to the top -- be the kind of reporter that *Time* valued most: someone who'd be encouraged to report not only the facts, but venture opinions about what the facts meant. So, in June 1961, with the help of Clare Booth Luce, I was more than ready for a tryout at *Time*.

I got it in San Francisco, where the bureau chief, T. George Harris, assigned me a story he couldn't seem to break loose. "Something called the Institute of Lay Theology at U.S.F.," he said. "Its director, a Jesuit named Gene Zimmers, won't even talk to me." Father Gene Zimmers was one of those young Jesuits who used to laugh and whine about trying to get things done in order. He'd been my best friend in the Society. Providence? I guess. I got the story. It ran long in the magazine, and Harris said I'd hit a home run my first at-bat in the major leagues.

When Richard N. Clurman, the chief of correspondents, brought me aboard in August (after almost three more months as a stringer in the Los Angeles bureau), he said he'd never send me to Rome because he was afraid of my Jesuit background. Six months later, I'd proven that my biases were identical to those of *Time* itself. *Time's* editors thought that the Church needed updating. So did I. So in late1961 they sent me to Rome, young wife and baby girl in tow, to cover the Council. Heady days.

First Day In Rome It would be an understatement to say that my Jesuit background helped me there. First day in town, I found California Jesuits getting their graduate degrees at the Gregorian University who were eager to tell me who was who at the Vatican. Soon, I got even better stuff from Father Edward Malatesta, a California Province classmate just finishing his theological studies at Chantilly near Paris. He phoned me one day to invite me to France for a crash course at the feet of the Church's most progressive theologians—mainly Jesuits and Dominicans and Benedictines who were mounting an attack on the stand-patters in the Roman Curia. These men were not only determined to help the pope take the Church back to a more primitive, more authentic, state—one that would be more Catholic, less Roman.

They knew they also had to mobilize public opinion, and, at that moment in history, they thought *Time* could help do that job. I returned from France with a three-month lead on all the other reporters in Rome. They knew there'd be a Council, but they didn't have a clue about the reformist spirit of the majority that would end up endowing the Church with a new charter, urging the people of God to roll up their sleeves and make the world a better place rather than stand apart from it. (The Church under Pius IX condemned the modern world as evil, and the world, for lack of a Christian presence, proved it by tumbling into two World Wars.)

By the time Pope John's Council began in October 1962, I had endeared myself to some of the Council's key theologians (called experts, or *periti*), simply because I was now one of the few reporters who understood where the pope and his collaborators wanted to lead. One of those *periti* was Roberto Tucci, the Jesuit who edited the semi-official Vatican journal of opinion, *Civiltá Cattolica*. Tucci met with the pope himself for editorial conferences every month; the pope liked to use *Civiltá* to float ideas he couldn't espouse openly himself. And Tucci—by a stroke of colossal luck—leaked all manner of information to me, stuff that *he* couldn't print in *Civiltá*.

Mere ex-Jesuit that I was, I suddenly had Jesuits all around me. The Jesuit ecumenist Gustave Weigel came to the Council as a *peritus* for the Secretariat for Promoting Christian Unity. He was our house guest for a few days before he found the proper digs. His boss, Cardinal Augustine Bea, was a Jesuit, too, and he and his staff became an important source for me.

I found yet a third Jesuit who helped me cover the Council, T.D. Roberts, the retired Archbishop of Bombay. I brought him home for dinner one night and he stayed for two years. My wife and I were thrilled. Monte Wooley could have played the part: the bishop who came to dinner—and stayed. That gave me another reportorial edge. Almost every day, Roberts brought home the conciliar handouts, documents labeled *Sub Secreto*. (They were all in Latin. But, as a Jesuit scholastic, I'd used Latin as a living language.)

Roberts handed me the documents with a conspiratorial smile, understanding as many Council Fathers did not, not then, that the media would force changes on the Church that the Roman Curia didn't want. Why? Because information itself subverted the power of power, by helping the people of God understand, and, by understanding, grow up into an adult faith. That's what Roberts wanted most: intelligent obedience to the Jesus message. His seminal book on authority, *Black Popes*, published in 1954, was really a plea for more democracy in the Church.

Before the Council, most Catholics had an image of the Church as a kind of pyramid, with the pope at the top (taking his cues directly from God), with the bishops just below taking their direction from the pope as a kind of CEO, then the priests, then the nuns, then the laity at the base of pyramid. It was the media coverage of this Council, the first Council in the history of the Church since the invention of radio and television (and newsmagazines), that changed that paradigm.. Though the Council sessions were supposed to be secret (because that's the way the Curia had set things up) reporters found ways to learn what was going on inside St. Peter's. And through these reporters the world learned that the bishops weren't there in Council to take directions from the pope. Rather, the pope told them he wanted them to help him figure out how he could move the barque of Peter (which had been in a kind of dry-dock) out on to the seas of the world. This, of course, gave my own spirit wings.

New View As a result, the Council began to look like any parliamentary body, full of factions, locked in argument, not about the overarching mission of the Church, but about the best ways of accomplishing that mission. The media seemed fascinated -- by the spectacle of one of the world's most ancient and conservative institutions beginning to change before the eyes of everyone who cared to pay attention. This Church wasn't looking much like a pyramid. Because reporters in Rome were doing their jobs, everyone could see that the Church was better imagined as a circle, a circle where everyone spoke, and everyone listened.

Gene Bianchi and I (and a couple dozen others) as Jesuit scholastics at St. Ignatius High in San Francisco, worked almost around the clock. Now, here in Rome, I was on the same kind of schedule. There were never enough hours. I'd have breakfast interviews, luncheon interviews, dinner interviews, midnight interviews.

One Sunday night, T.D. Roberts invited some other bishops to dinner, and some Jesuits from the Gregorian University showed up, too, in greater numbers than my wife and I had counted on. So, instead of a sit down dinner for eight, we had a buffet supper for a dozen. "That was fun," said my wife, Sue. "Let's do this more often." So we began to have a buffet supper every Sunday night, the more the merrier. Other bishops and theologians started inviting their friends and the numbers grew. Sunday nights at the Kaiser's—with dozens of the Council's progressive leaders there in force—became an institution at the Council. Henry Luce paid for it all, of course, and he couldn't have been more pleased.

At one point, I brought Gene Bianchi to Rome, and made him a well-paid stringer so he, with his fluency in Italian and his understanding of the Church, could help Bob Elson, a senior writer from New York, do the Vatican interviews he needed for his text piece in *LIFE*. They attempted to see the pope, but all they got was a 15-second pep talk.

Elson brightened when I took him to my interview with John XXIII, arranged by Cardinal Francis Spellman in return for a loan from *Time* of its "Illuminations" of the Sistine Chapel, which Spellman used in his Vatican Pavilion at the New York World's Fair. Popes didn't give interviews then, and this one wasn't official. Accidentally on purpose, John XXIII wandered up a hallway at Castel Gondolfo one summer morning a couple months before the Council and ran into me and Elson, chatting with the pope's personal private executive secretary, Loris Capovilla. We thought we would get maybe 30 seconds with John XXIII. He kept us for almost an hour. He had things to tell *Time* (and *LIFE*), but they weren't churchy things. He wanted to talk politics, geo-politics, and he did.

This made a church story into something more than that. This was still the middle of the Cold War, and the Soviet Union and the U.S. were threatening to blow up the world with their nuclear arms and their deadly missiles. Dumb idea, said Pope John, and he was inclined to blame the Church and the U.S. for pursuing this dumb idea to an absurdity, which is what he named the "holy war against Communism." This was a holy war? Yes, said the pope. "Like the Crusades. And we don't want any more crusades." So what was the Church to do? "Get people together," said the pope, "help them emphasize what unites us as human beings, not focus on what divides us."

Key Story Later, after the pope had left, Capovilla told us a story— about a visit the pope had had from a group of Calvinists from Taizé in France.

"Why can't we get together?" John XXIII said to the visitors.

"We have different ideas," said their leader.

John XXIII laughed. "Ideas, ideas, what are ideas among friends?"

I gasped. Since 1937, churchmen had been pushing fear and hatred of all kinds of "isms"—Communism, atheism, Protestantism. Now here was a pope daring not to deal with abstract "isms," but proposing instead that people stop trying to destroy one another and start paying more attention to the common humanity in everyone. In a few months, this pope would come out with an encyclical that spelled out this notion in fuller detail. It was called *Pacem In Terris*, Peace on Earth.

My editors in New York gasped, too. "You can't tell me," cabled Henry Grunwald, then *Time*'s foreign editor, "that the Church has dropped its stance as a bulwark against Communism." In a series of cables over the next few months, reporting story after story about the pope's reaching out to leaders on the other side of the so-called Iron Curtain, I tried to tell him exactly that. In October 1962, I reported how Pope John XXIII intervened in the Cuba-missile crisis and mediated a kind of standoff between Nikita Khrushchev and President John Kennedy. Maybe those stories had some effect. At the beginning of 1963, at any rate, *Time* declared Pope John XXIII "Man of the Year."

At the approach of the new millennium, I was hoping that *Time* would name John XXIII and Mikhail Gorbachev as men of the century. They had each turned two monoliths around. Pope John made the Church more free, more human, more loving, more humble in the face of history. And President Gorbachev made peace (after a fashion) among nations, and almost single-handedly ended the Cold War. If I'd stayed at *Time*—one of my life's few regrets is that I didn't— I might have been able to make a case. I'm not sure how effectively I could have done that. But it doesn't really matter. For a time, I was a secret Jesuit, open to the winds of change, with a vision of my own— that I could help tell stories that would popularize new paradigms of church and state, and possibly even make the world a better place.

Sounds goody-goody, doesn't it? But it was what I did. And it was me. I don't know if it was the Holy Spirit that impelled me, but my reportage was passionate, creative, innovative, propelling, driving, pushing. And my Jesuit friends told me that this reporting opened the hearts and minds of millions around the world.

I don't know about that. But I know that if *Time* hadn't paid me, I would have paid *Time*. It was that much fun.

And the fun of it all grooved me for the rest of my life. I kept looking for new waves to ride, new ideas to report on, new heroes -- and heroines -- to celebrate.

(*Robert Blair Kaiser is an author, playwright and journalist, an expert on current affairs in the Catholic Church.*)

Chapter Ten

Two Roads Diverged

James Torrens

*Spiritual paths begin together,
then diverge.*

L
ife stories do not unfold independently of one another. To reflect on my own life story, in the context of this volume, entwines me immediately with that of Eugene Bianchi. We were in close contact for about twenty-five years, from age 14 to age 40. In our school years we poured over the same books and absorbed the same influences, which can be summed up pretty well in the term given to our high school teachers, "Jesuit scholastics." These young men, not yet ordained priests, were imbued (some more than others, of course) by the philosophy of St. Thomas Aquinas, the medieval teacher par excellence. The scholastics—or "Misters," as we called them—belonged to a Catholic religious order dedicated to the imitation of Jesus according to a pattern of prayer, the Spiritual Exercises, devised by the founder, Saint Ignatius of Loyola.

In my Junior and Senior years at Saint Ignatius High School, San Francisco, 1946-48, I met up frequently with Gene Bianchi as we came and went, in our Junior jackets, from two office doors facing one another, that of *The Red and Blue*, the school newspaper, and that of *The Ignatian*, the newsmagazine and yearbook. In his senior year, Gene became editor of *The Red and Blue* and I of *The Ignatian*. Our Italian roots, shared also by most of the editors, added to the affinity. I can remember Gene once chatting in Genoese with a few of these young men, fellow commuters with him from Oakland. This intrigued me, because I could not venture past the school Italian my mother taught me. Our mothers, incidentally, came later to be friends. In those formative years, Gene Bianchi and I did not appreciate our pedagogical good luck. We had the blessing of intelligent and energetic teachers only a decade older than ourselves, and they fed us out of a stream of brand new, high-quality textbooks by young Jesuit authors—the Latin series by the "Mister" Robert Henle, taking us into Cicero and Virgil; the Prose and Poetry series by Julian Maline and others, with its generous sampling of English and American classics; an introduction to Homeric Greek by Raymond Schoeder, full of photos and classical lore. What a lot of memorizing we did in those days, focused as we were upon that impossible ideal, eloquentia perfecta.

I had a flair for writing, which I got to indulge under the tutelage of "Mister" Eugene Zimmers, who turned our Ignatian magazine into a look-alike for *Time*. Imitation of models was understood to be the way to learn to write, and Mr. Zimmers had us studying and copying the purplish prose that constituted Time-style. Gene, as I recall it, took more to the spoken word. He became prominent in speech contests and Shakespearean events. In our early seminary studies, his poise and delivery earned him the title role in our class production of Coriolanus, just the thing for an all-male cast but woefully short on show-stopper scenes. I looked young for my years in those days and did not have much of a voice, so I did not figure in the casting. (The only time I ever appeared in a play, as I now love to recount, was in the sixth grade, for an allegorical piece on safety procedures where I had one line: "I am the reckless pedestrian.")

Joining the Jesuits In 1948, Gene and I, with two classmates, went straight off from high school to the Jesuit novitiate, in a car driven by our high school chaplain, Father Alexander Cody. We were full of good will and mostly innocent of the world. My mother's concern about my "going overboard" religiously was soon borne out. Those were strict days in the religious orders, with a lot of silence to be observed, when necessary communication had to be in Latin, no matter how barbarous, the daily order was tight, and we had lots of rules whose relative importance was not easy for all to sort out.

Robert Coles recently, in *The Secular Mind*, talked about this earlier era as productive of "children deeply afraid of doing the wrong thing, or worried that they might slip up"—or, I suppose, in religious terms, worried about offending God and going to hell. I can recognize myself there. Now we have the opposite extreme, says Coles, "what has become mentioned by more and more of us in our clinical case studies, the 'narcissistic personality.'" Both of these groups can tend to the same religious goal—a mature, confident belief, with capacity for loving concern—but without a doubt they start from opposite points.

Our Master of Novices, Father Francis Seeliger, was an old hand in Jesuit administration, with a falsely gruff manner and a love of physical projects for us to execute. We spent each October of those years in the vineyards getting in the harvest for Novitiate Wines, an interlude we welcomed. The pickers divided roughly into the speedsters, whom we called "hooters"—my memory puts Gene among them—and those of us who were left in the dust.

How latinate all our studies were. Even for English composition and speaking, we took as model John Henry Newman who, with the page-long sentences of his oration "The Second Spring," led us into the thickets of Ciceronian periodical style. After that, it took me years to limber up my writing or coax it to a more Attic simplicity. Our three years of philosophy study initiated us to the thesis method where, for our examinations, we had to explain and defend, in Latin, a bevy of propositions in epistemology, metaphysics, cosmology, natural theology. We approached each thesis with a bristling list of adversaries. Thomas Aquinas was the authority, the one with the final say, though with Aristotle often enough standing firmly behind him.

We did, I remember, have one very good Introduction to Modern Philosophy, from Father Edmund Morton, with a textbook in hand written by James Collins of St. Louis University. I remember writing an 'A' paper on Kant's Critique of the Aesthetic Judgment without really comprehending what I was talking about. Our contemporary lights in those years were Gilson, Maritain and, just emerging, Bernard Lonergan, S.J. During our third year, at Mount St. Michael's philosophate outside Spokane, Gene represented the rest of the seminarians before the house administration as what we called "beadle."

Mostly, though not entirely, he carried messages down rather than up.

Between 1955-58, Gene and I put in three years of high-school teaching, like the "Misters" who had formed us. I spent the first two of them in a minor seminary for the diocese of Monterey-Fresno, which the Jesuits conducted during the Fifties, and then joined him as a teacher at our alma mater, St. Ignatius High.

Then, thanks to capacity enrollment in our own school of theology, Alma College in the Santa Cruz Mountains of California—thanks also to some forward-looking superiors—Gene and I and a third companion, a leading light of our class, Edward Malatesta, went off to Europe on the ocean liner Saturnia, to stay for four years with no interim returns. Malatesta settled into park-like surroundings in Chantilly, France, while Gene and I found ourselves amidst Flanders fields just outside Louvain, in Belgium. We were all three ordained after our third year of study, Gene and I at the Jesuit church in Brussels, an occurrence no doubt bitter-sweet for him because his parents could not afford the trip.

Stretching the Rope   Gene, I must confess, proved the best of us at stretching the very short rope we were given for travel. After our second year of studies in Europe, we were supposed to spend the summer close to home, a summer of British Channel weather where my asthma quickly kicked in. Gene went to bat for me with the house administration and sprung me for the most beautiful respite of my life, three weeks in a guest cabin of some teaching sisters above Bellagio, Lake Como, in Italy. He did me less of a favor a year later, after our ordination, coming home from Spain with hepatitis, which two of us Americans picked up from him. It knocked me out of action for ten weeks of melancholy, dozing and reading, especially *Brothers Karamazov*.

Those years in Belgium broadened us provincial Californians greatly, despite all the inefficiencies and rigidities we found. Much more relevantly, there was theological ferment. True, we still had interminable classes and mounds of mimeographed notes in Latin. But our teachers were propounding the primacy of charity in moral theology, the sacraments as Christological and ecclesial encounters, the scriptures as products of an inspired process of shaping and editing, the Anglican preachers as a guide to our own preaching.

These were the years, 1958-62, that prepared the surprises of Vatican Council II. Our professors, in the midst of their own aggiornamento, looked warily at the announcement of a council, afraid of some serious clamping down. We had been meanwhile imbibing an exciting theology of the resurrection from Durrwell and Cerfaux, a vision of the laity's role in the church from Congar, an appreciation of the patristic era from De Lubac, and above all an understanding of how grace acts within and upon nature as drawn from Malevez (Leopold Malevez, our own senior professor) and from Karl Rahner. Rahner's abundant writings, then and later, marked me for life.

Gene Bianchi, in those years, impressed us with his journalistic initiatives: interviews with some leading lights on church renewal in Latin America or in the church as a whole. He had "push," which was not exactly pleasing to those anxious to contain us. I remember a three-day Easter vacation over the border of Belgium to Amiens and Rouen, which we had to stretch into four-day because of a railroad strike at the border. We were not exactly welcomed home. Gene, more than myself, was heading out onto a sea of wide contacts, reportorial inquiry and engagement with the spirit of the times. Ecumenical concerns would take him later through Union Theological Seminary and mark his collaboration, at Santa Clara University, with Professor and Presbyterian minister Stuart MacLean. During restive times, as director of the Center for the Study of Contemporary Values, he stirred the pot too at Santa Clara by initiating a Marxist-Christian dialogue with Roger Garaudy, something unheard of in those days.

I later went in some of the directions Gene had explored. My own graduate studies at the University of Michigan opened up a number of welcome ecumenical contacts. In the mid-1970's, I set about to learn Spanish, which then allowed me travel and immersion in Mexico, Central and South America , so that I could later spend much of the Nineties reporting on church and other sectors of Latin America for the Jesuit weekly America. Gene himself had served on America long before me while a graduate student in New York at Union Theological Seminary. Even Gene's departure from the Jesuits and marriage, taking him to Emory University, Atlanta, did not at first distance us much, because I taught for two years, 1968-70, just across the border in Alabama, at Tuskegee Institute.

Roads Diverge But Gene was by this time moving beyond the parameters within which I have continued to live. I must admit now, way down the road of my own Jesuit life, to reading some of his position statements and wondering how we got so far apart. It is not that we were out of touch. Gene, with his gift for friendship, has managed to keep periodically in communication, despite one or another of my messages of dismay, after reading what he has said to members of CORPUS (priests not now officially active) or perusing some stricture of his against a celibate priesthood.

Luke Timothy Johnson, the New Testament scholar and one of Gene's colleagues at Emory, may have shed some light on our differing paths in his recent book, *Living Jesus*. In discussing "the decision to learn Jesus within the framework of the tradition of the church," Johnson also talks of "the risk involved." He contends that "the willingness to learn Jesus in the context of tradition demands a combination of loyalty and criticism," and states that "either without the other becomes distorted." "Loyalty," he says, "is ideally the premise for true criticism, just as critical awareness is a necessary component of loyalty." The loyalty runs the risk of hardening into "established formulas about Jesus or ossified interpretations of him." The criticism, for its part, needs the boundary that Johnson calls "the loss of a certain autonomy."

I confess myself a loyalist. I don't know about "established formulas" or "ossified interpretations," but I do know about my own lapses of courage—understandable but grievous in this terrible century—and I recognize my failures to see clear, or look steadily enough, on various issues. But I have no hesitancy about remaining Catholic with a capital 'c,' without prejudice, I hope, to the rest of the world. The church is certainly often a mixed bag. But to think of it as a construct of early leaders, or as my own to dictate to, or take liberties with (as distinct from representing difficulties and throwing up the hands in some frustration), I can't go that route, that "road."

"Religio," etymologically and in my own understanding, means commitment before it means explanation. Generalizations about "world religion," if it relativizes one's own faith, does a disservice. And as to Jesus Christ, a universalist (or "transtraditional") approach to him as "a Jewish sage" and world religious figure instead of as risen Savior, head of the Body of the faithful, source of grace, a name by which alone we may be saved—that leaves me shaking my head. No dechristifying, please, of the divine milieu.

I know that I cannot just end like that. I have to express my respect, and even wonderment, at a friend who has read and thought so widely, faced into the wind of contemporary issues, labored long, and given of himself graciously to so many students. He has reached a peak of accomplishment, and this volume pays tribute to that.

New Plans As for me, I have enjoyed a decade as a Catholic journalist, plus theater reviewer and occasional poet. And I have a small Sunday congregation, with its Baptist or evangelical component, where I feel at times surprisingly at home, though at times full of puzzlement. For my parishioners are prisoners, i.e., guests of the New York state correctional system, and psychiatric patients as well, which puts them in the worst of double binds. I am moving soon, however, to Tijuana, Mexico, to get back into some college teaching and chaplaincy in my later years, with fellow Jesuits, in a milieu with huge elemental needs but a no less real demand for thoughtful, principled and skilled professionals and public servants.

Gene Bianchi has written with feeling and comprehension about the waning years of life. In his book *Aging as a Spiritual Journey* (Crossroad, 1984), he interviewed elders who were notable for their initiative, optimism and depth of spirit. I would hope to be one of those. Saint Bonaventure, that second founder of the Franciscans, wrote: "A spiritual joy is the greatest sign of the divine grace dwelling in a soul." That is the message enshrined in the "Magnificat" of the Virgin Mary; it was the theme of my last annual retreat. I have been enabled to pass my recent years pretty much in that way and would hope to continue doing so, with an awareness of the divine presence.

The divine presence, which sometimes does strike me as in the Mexican triangular motif, *el ojo de Dios* (the eye of God), is still by far best typified for me in the imagery and scriptural wording associated with "the Sacred Heart of Jesus." It is a real presence, actuated for the Christian community in the daily Eucharist, which continues to be of central importance to me. So I guess my road has been a very traditional Catholic one.

All my life, however, I have been a resolute hiker, in the California Sierras and elsewhere. When off in the woods, I have appreciated whoever fell in with me to walk along for a while before branching off, as well as whoever, taking another trail, has somewhere crossed back to encounter my own. In the case of Gene Bianchi, both of the above circumstances apply.

I have also continued to practice as a poet and thus to keep thinking figuratively, which explains my choice of a Robert Frost allusion to sum up our two lives in the woods—Dantean woods?--of the late twentieth century. "Two roads diverged in a yellow wood. . . .and that has made all the difference."

(James Torrens, a Jesuit priest, is a journalist and a poet.)

Intermezzo III

Story telling...is holy.

The very act of storytelling, of arranging memory and invention according to the structure of narrative, is by definition holy. It is a version, however finite, of what the infinite God does. Telling our stories is what saves us; the story is enough. . . .

James Carroll

Chapter Eleven

Teaching 'Great Books' as Spiritual Practice

Wendy Farley

*Dialoguing with texts transforms
a spirituality*

Among my academic tasks is to teach the "great books" of western thought to undergraduates and to graduate students. And I feel myself possessed and shaped in my spirituality by these works in a way that belies their status simply as a history of thought. This phenomenon creates for me a welcome opportunity to reflect on the relationship between spiritual life and academic vocation, and I will do so not so much by talking about my own autobiography, but rather by describing the intellectual practice that connects my *self* to the thinkers I teach.

One of the main practices a theologian engages in, of course, is reading the works of other theologians. This practice functions in many ways in any one person's life and in many ways in the history of theology and academics. I have come to understand it as a version of Platonic dialectic.

Dialectic is notoriously ill-defined even in the texts wherein it is mentioned directly (e.g., Plato's *Republic* and *Sophist*; Plotinus's first Ennead). It seems to point to a practice by which the intellect and reason are trained to discern and experience ever more directly the nature of reality. The practice may be structured as a study of a particular intellectual lineage, narrowly: the works of Plato and perhaps a few other Platonists (especially Plotinus) and Christian neoplatonists (Pseudo-Dionysius, Origen, Anselm, Nicolas of Cusa and so on). But less narrowly considered, it is the study of any of those lineages of religious thought through which the desire to contemplate reality takes a philosophical form. In my own case, this has come to include an amateur study of Tibetan Buddhism. Thus the study of other thinkers' writings becomes the occasion for trying to taste not only the thought but the reality which they all tried to corral into prose.

It might become clearer what dialectic is by first distinguishing it from what it is not. It is not simply an academic study of a history of ideas, interpreted well or badly by succeeding scholars. I am always a little challenged when teaching Bonaventure's *The Soul's Journey into God*, because he begins by dissuading readers from undertaking study at all if they believe that "reading is sufficient without unction, speculation without devotion, investigation without wonder." There is, of course, a legitimate practice of scholarship which approaches the "great books" of western thought in this way, "without devotion." This very acceptable form of study is not what I mean by dialectic.

Neither is the practice of dialectic an attachment to one school of thought with the idea that it enjoys possession of the correct metaphysical portrait of reality. A platonist in this sense would stray from the desire for truth, instead substituting a conceptual system for reality itself.

The practice of dialectic I speak of is a passionate, dedicated, energetic devotion to rigorous understanding of the whole intellectual lineage of which it is a part. It must be at the same time an understanding, or better, an experience, of the non-identity between any word, concept, or metaphysical scheme and the truth to which it attempts to point. The practice requires, for instance, that one study the ideas of Plato, Plotinus, Pseudo-Dionysius, Nicolas of Cusa and so on *as if* everything depended on the clearest and most precise understanding of these ideas possible.

The practice of dialectic is carried out best in a community of inquiry, that is, as teachers and students struggle together to understand the ideas of the texts they share. It is necessarily a dialogical practice. Certainly an enormous amount of intellectual effort occurs in one's own head: the reading of texts itself and the struggle to understand what one is reading, reflection on the ideas, ancillary practices of meditation or contemplation that all occur in the lonely and quiet parts of the soul. But in the absence of dialogue and community, the practice itself is quite truncated. This is partly because of the limited nature of any single person's mind. One cannot think of everything oneself. Hauling into words, ideas, and arguments what one has partially seen in a text—in the presence of others—is a method for making one's own apprehension of the insight much deeper and more stable. One's own understanding is then deepened as these efforts are subject to augmentation, affirmation, and criticism by colleagues.

Perhaps even more than this, however, is the way in which dialogue mirrors the fundamentally relational structure of reality. One of the central insights of dialectic is that everything is related to everything else. This insight can be arrived at only superficially in a practice that is isolated from others.

Reality Not Conceptual At the same time, the non-conceptual nature of reality is one of its most decisive features. This means that dialectic is the training of reason, which is by its nature structured by the correlation between concept and being, to apprehend reality that is beyond being and beyond concept. The process by which a faculty structured so rigidly first by sense experience and then by reason's relationship to being can be freed from this structure occurs only gradually. It does so by walking the way of discursive reason which correlates being and reason as carefully and deeply as possible. This is why the study of philosophy and metaphysics was the first and is still the very appropriate subject matter of academia.

A first step in dialectic is the struggle of discursive reason to understand ideas. But the ideas present in philosophy function as a conceptual discourse that then explodes conceptual discourse. Reading Pseudo-Dionysius's *Divine Names* and *Mystical Theology* is simultaneously a study of abstract metaphysics and a practice that uses reason to surpass reason and enter "the way of unknowing."

Another example of this would be trying to think the metaphysical attributes of God as they are laid out in the *Summa Theologica* of Thomas Aquinas. It is a somewhat difficult exercise (at least to those of us who are a little slow in this regard) simply to read and understand the words and arguments by which God is described as simple, good, infinite, immutable, eternal, a unity and so on. But then one must begin to think these not as names or concepts of God but as negations of attributes: they are primarily the withholding of attributes rather then the designating of attributes to God.

Immutability, for example, withholds from God certain very specific ways that finite beings are subject to change. The mind must now stretch itself to understand not the words or the arguments Aquinas lays out, but the actual content of the ideas. What is simplicity, how can such a concept be thought? It is actually rather difficult to think "simplicity": not just arguments about it but the thing itself (at least, since this is an autobiographical sketch, it is difficult for me).

But even this is not enough; one must think not only what phenomena like simplicity, immutability, unity are, but also what is this mode of reality, this God, that can be named only through these negations? One must think beyond the meaning of simplicity, immutability and so on to a reality that requires these as its names. Or rather, one's mind must reach for a mode of reality whose attributes are all non-attributes: not simply negations absolutely but negations of all the ways in which any thinkable reality which has any kind of being in any way must exist.

Beyond Contradiction   Thinking the divine attributes is to use discursive reasoning so that one is pushed beyond its scope. At the edge of this form of reasoning, something else opens. It is not, according to the bifurcating logic of modernity, an object of "faith" or just an emotional experience. It is precisely what opens to the intellect as it pushes to its upward capacity, its capacity not only for being but for truth or wisdom. As Nicolas of Cusa puts it, beyond the wall of contradiction lies paradise. In the platonic tradition, this is not the surrender of reason, but precisely what is illuminated by the practice of dialectic.

Dialectic takes truth itself, in its purest and most immediate form, as its object. Although it requires the exercise of what might be called academic forms of reasoning (close textual interpretation, following and developing arguments, and so on), these are themselves only instruments or tools, indispensable but insufficient.

It is desire rather than the analytical skills reason can acquire that directs the human being toward reality itself. Aristotle begins his metaphysics by attesting to this most basic desire: all human beings "by nature desire to know." Also a ruthlessly honest disposition is indispensable for this practice, in order to avoid stalling out on mere appearance.

One's practice will be correlatively compromised as it is tainted by either an acceptance of the line of thought as authoritative in and of itself or by a desire to find security or consolation in a particular world-view. For instance, it is the strongly critical edge to dialectic that contributes to its usefulness to a feminist (as counter-intuitive as it may seem at the outset). A lack of attachment to an authoritative tradition, even as one is shaped by its wisdom, enables one to discover and reject remnants of sexism and patriarchy present in it. As the desire for truth is distracted by competing desires for the security of an authoritative tradition or a "consoling fiction" (Murdoch), its pursuit is weakened and muddied.

The relationship between eros and truth is probably dialectical as well: as one approaches truth, the desire for it is purified and intensified. Desire finds itself gradually freed from the distractions of competing desires. But it is the birth of the desire for truth itself that makes dialectic possible at all. However mixed, however wrongly directed, if the desire for truth is born in even the smallest way in a person, all of the penultimate attachments gradually fall away and the luminosity of truth begins dawn in the soul.

For me, studying and teaching the texts of neoplatonism has been a way of integrating dimensions of spiritual life with my academic vocation. The interconnections between philosophical theology and contemplation were made more explicit for me in my study of Tibetan Buddhism. Through a series of accidents, I found myself working with a Tibetan monk and scholar. With him I studied in an informal way the religious practices and philosophical thought of

Tibetan Buddhism and also with a Rizong Rinpoche, who taught in Atlanta for a year. I was very struck by a contrast I found between western religious philosophical thought and that of Tibetan Buddhism. In the latter, the meditation practices and philosophy are taught together, as two interdependent dimensions of understanding reality. In studying mahamudra, for example, we listened to quite rigorous philosophical descriptions about the nature of reality as empty and "merely imputed." But the last third of each session was dedicated to a meditation that was related to the teaching. We were in this way bringing both discursive and non-discursive forms of analysis to bear on the subject matter. In the Gelukpa branch of Tibetan Buddhism, this interdependence of scholarship and meditation is understood to be a very formidable combination of practices aimed at attaining the bodhisattva ideal.

Soul Becomes a Flame Experiencing the intimacy between metaphysics and meditation in Tibetan Buddhism sent me back to the western philosophical and theological traditions with new eyes. It occurred to me that in the great texts of neoplatonism, Hellenistic and Christian alike, the same interdependence is presupposed. The primary difference is that the techniques of meditation or contemplation are rarely recommended in the texts. They appear only indirectly, as when Plotinus describes the Good: "Then of it and of itself the soul has all the vision that may be—of itself luminous now, filled with intellectual light, become pure light, subtle and weightless. It has become divine, is part of the eternal that is beyond becoming. It is like a flame." A passage like this is intended as metaphysics. And yet, the metaphysics and epistemology presupposes something like direct experience of non-conceptual reality which has then tried to find its way into language.

My encounter with Tibetan Buddhism has proven infinitely helpful to me at many levels, including the way it opened up my own intellectual and spiritual tradition for me. I find the bifurcations imposed by modernity between reason and emotion, religion and philosophy, faith and reason, subjective and objective, mind and body to be more and more distorting and even destructive. The interdependence of all of the activities I engage in, the various dimensions of my academic and spiritual and interpersonal life has come into somewhat clearer focus.

I am grateful to Gene Bianchi for being among the pioneers of scholars who have tried to be very explicit in his linking of scholarship and spiritual life and finding creative ways of incorporating these links into his teaching and scholarship. On the eve of his retirement, I am honored to add my voice to many others in thanking him for his life's work.

(*Wendy Farley, an author and theologian, teaches at Emory University.*)

Chapter Twelve

FROM *Wissenschaft*
TO THEOLOGY
David R. Blumenthal

*A scholar seeks God in a century
of atrocities*

The following narrative is an old family story. One Rosh ha-Shana, at about age three or four, I was standing with my mother in the congregation of which my father was the rabbi while the cantor was saying *kiddush*. It was 1941 or 1942 in Houston, Texas, and the service was very formal: robes for the rabbi and cantor, a choir, and an organ. As the cantor sang the kiddush, I turned to my mother and asked, "Is that God?"

In retrospect, that story expresses the tone and quality of my life's work, and in two ways. First, the question of my life has always been, "Is that God?" Is God the majestic creator of Genesis, or is God the powerful redeemer of the Exodus? Is God the comforting presence of Psalms, or is God the demanding yet fair father of the ten commandments and the laws? Is God "Yahweh" of academic biblical scholarship, or is God "Hashem" of Jewish piety? Second, the story, my story, approaches the problem of who God is from the point of view of wonder. It is personal spiritual experience that is the springboard for the question and the ultimate judge of the answer for, although the appeal is to my mother, it is I who will have to hear and weigh the answer.

Strangely, I never had any formal or informal instruction on ideas about God or relationship with God. My education in Jewish parochial schools never dealt with God, a fact at which Christians may wonder, but that is how it is in Jewish schools. We teach texts and culture, we practice liturgy, and we are active in politics and social justice causes. But we do not talk about God and spiritual awareness. My father, in spite of the fact that he was a rabbi, never talked about God or prayer. The professional cantor who sang in his synagogue had great volume but no inwardness. It was only when my father acted as cantor that I was able to hear him actually pray and, then, I heard a man who had a deep personal relationship with God, who sang to God, and who sang for God's people to God. I learned more by listening and watching than by being instructed.

The world around me couldn't have cared less about God. My childhood peers were interested in games. My teenage and college peers were interested in women and grades. And my adult peers have been interested in building institutions, money, vacations, family, and all the many other preoccupations of the "real" world. Who thinks of God, especially in the Jewish community where issues of survival and continuity are paramount? I was probably the only person in that childhood synagogue to wonder if the cantor was God; perhaps I still am.

Meanwhile, my Jewish identity began to take on form. I went to a Jewish day school (a parochial high school) and began to learn the basic texts. I can still recite whole sections of Isaiah, Jeremiah, and the other prophets. What power! The Hebrew is so lapidary, the imagery so forceful, the challenge to society on behalf of God so absolute! I remember, too, modern Hebrew literature. The poetry teacher would read, the lunch bell would sound, and no one would move until he had finished. There was riveting power in the story of the people but there was no mention of God or of social justice.

During this period I became a reconstructionist. I read many of the works of Mordecai Kaplan and used the *Reconstructionist Prayerbook* in my daily worship. This prayerbook deletes all references to the personal messiah, the resurrection, the sacrifices, and the chosenness of the Jewish people. God was the "power that made for salvation," in Kaplan's inimitable phrase. New prayers and liturgical formulations are substituted, and I used them in personal devotions, though I was being trained in an Orthodox day school and prayed in a Conservative synagogue on Shabbat and holidays. I remember, too, the vote in the United Nations in November 1947 and the establishment of the State of Israel in May 1948. For years, teenage extracurricular energies were devoted to the Zionist movement: to studying the pioneers and to dreaming of going to Israel.

An Honor to Study Judaism The academic study of Jewish civilization, Wissenschaft des Judentums, did not begin for me until I reached college, and I fell for it hook, line, and sinker. It was an honor to take graduate courses at the University of Pennsylvania, even as a freshman, with men who were legends in their own lifetimes. I read Genesis with E. A. Speiser while he was composing the Anchor Bible commentary. I studied the Dead Sea Scrolls with Y. Kutscher during the colorful professional dispute over the possibility of the scrolls being medieval forgeries. I read Qoran and "The Thousand and One Nights" in Arabic with S. D. Goitein while he was composing his great work on Jewish life under Islam. And I studied Ezekiel with M. Greenberg while he was writing his two volume commentary on that book. I could tell many stories about these men. The élan of being in the inner group of the best oriental studies department in the western hemisphere was very seductive. Being able to spend all day Saturday in the oriental studies seminar library following footnotes and checking sources was very appealing. Writing an honors thesis and publishing my first article were a privilege.

My college years at the University of Pennsylvania also saw the fulfillment of my Zionist dream. I spent a year in Israel. In those days, a trip to Israel was not a summer outing; it was an ideological act. The trip was by boat and we built up to our arrival with song, dance, and ideological study. Once arrived, the conditions were primitive. We could see the Jordanian gun emplacements from our dormitory windows. We visited and stayed on kibbutzim where we argued socialism, capitalism, democracy, politics, the meaning of Jewish history, and of course *aliyah*, that is, settlement in the land as the only true form of Jewish identity. We also took our turn in the barns, kitchens, and on night guard duty. There was no western wall to go to in 1958-59 and, if Jerusalem was orthodox, I did not know it. The University of Pennsylvania and the State of Israel in the 1950's were not the place to ask, "Is that God?" Rather, life was framed by scholarly, historical, and ideological issues.

Having been swept off my feet by *Wissenschaft des Judentums* and pioneering Zionism, I returned to America and went to the Jewish Theological Seminary. I was in what was the (unofficial) scholarly track. In preparation for my masters exam, I read through most of the Tanakh excerpting the quotable quotations. At the Seminary, I again studied with men who were legends in their lifetimes. I studied Jewish history with Salo Baron while he was still writing his multi-volume history. I read Jeremiah with Shalom Spiegel, who radiated scholarly and linguistic elegance, and Job with Robert Gordis while he was writing his book on that subject. I studied Talmud with Saul Lieberman, the outstanding academic talmudist of the century, and with David Weiss-Halivni. And I worked with Max Kadushin, one of the most interesting though neglected minds in the area of rabbinic scholarship. For all of these men, the academic study of Judaism was a way of life. They were also traditional Jews, but it was their study of the sources that counted. This is best illustrated by a widely known *bon mot*: "Mysticism is foolishness but the study of mysticism is academic." Only Heschel was different, but I did not study with him at the Seminary.

The Seminary years again found me in Israel. This time I was more aware of spiritual issues though, again, it was the Zionist-pioneering problems that were predominant. The Seminary years also introduced me to Zalmen Schachter. "Reb Zalmen," as he was known to us, came from a Hasidic background, wandered into contemporary eastern spirituality and other things, and dealt in spiritual psychodrama. He taught us about spiritual prayer and some of us formed a break-away morning service where we actually prayed instead of reciting the liturgy. My attempt to bring some of that insight back into the regular Seminary service led to a sharp reprimand. Rabbinical School and the State of Israel in the 1960's were not the place to ask, "Is that God?" Rather, again, life was framed by scholarly, historical, and ideological issues.

If I had thought that the active rabbinate was the place to ask my question, I was wrong there too. My four years in the pulpit were filled with professional tasks: programming, preaching, pastoral work, education, political action, administration, and community politics. I was good at some of this—primarily the teaching, preaching, and pastoral work—but the rest was not my forte. The congregation was wonderful. I left in good graces and still return there occasionally. But it was a time of isolation from my academic Jewish identity, although actually being a rabbi—in the pulpit and in the social role —engendered a practical kind of spiritual growth. During my years in the rabbinate, I married and we began raising a family. These have been a source of much support to me, then as now.

Return to Studies A return to doctoral studies seemed to be the best path. My doctoral program at Columbia University, however, was a great disappointment. There was no real instruction in history of religions, only one superficial survey course. The New Testament courses were all tendentiously Christian. There was no student teaching and no preparing of syllabi. However, the program left me free to do what I really wanted to do—read medieval Jewish texts. So, I read philosophic texts from the beginning to the end, together with the secondary literature, and wrote and passed my doctoral exams. For my thesis, I again worked with a man who was a legend in his own lifetime. Georges Vajda of Paris was a world-class authority on Islam, and on Jewish philosophy and mysticism. A very unprepossessing man, Vajda had a knowledge that was so vast that, when he retired, it took fourteen of us to replace him. He was la science juive in Europe after the war.

The result of my doctoral work was two books and several essays—each rich in edited texts, learned footnotes, and seminal scholarly hypotheses—and a career in medieval Judaism. Studying the intersection of Jewish philosophy, mysticism, and traditional rabbinic theology was finally a good place to ask, "Is that God?" especially since philosophy and mysticism claim to have definitive answers to that question. It was also a safe place to be: analyzing and writing footnotes about works written hundreds of years ago when people still believed in ptolemaic astronomy, spontaneous generation, and mono-cultural truth.

Neusner's Influence   It was Jacob Neusner who opened my eyes to what I was really doing. While teaching with him at Brown University, Neusner asked me to teach what I knew: Jewish mysticism. I said it could not be done because the material was very complex and besides there were no texts in English. "So, translate them," he replied, "A teacher must be able to teach what he knows." As my two volumes of Understanding Jewish Mysticism evolved, Neusner asked, "Why would anyone want to study this?" So I had to become explicit about the nature of spirituality, the difference between spirituality and mysticism, and the various types of Jewish mysticism. I thought my work was pellucid but Jack would say, "I don't understand this. Did you show it to your wife? Did she understand it?" So I rewrote, many times, getting more explicit and clearer each time.

Neusner's other contribution to my professional life came in requesting a syllabus on modern Judaism. I rewrote the syllabus several times and, eventually, got the point: Judaism was not just what the duly authorized rabbis and thinkers were saying; it was what the people were doing. Even more important: most of "Judaism" was not religious, and certainly not spiritual, much less philosophic or mystical. Secular forms of Judaism were, in fact and much to my surprise, the norm. It was not the others who were not "with it"; it was I who was not "with it." And they were no less legitimately Jewish than I. In fact, Jewish identity through culture, history, and polity was a way of being Jewish unto itself and the academic study of Judaism, which had become my way of life and from which I was making my living, was the key to this secular Jewish identity. Brown University was not the place to ask, "Is that God?" but it was a good place to ask, in full self-consciousness, "What substitutes for God?"

In spite of my growing academic commitments, which I now realized were really ideological, I enrolled my children in Jewish day schools and prayed in an Orthodox synagogue, though I kept my Conservative affiliations. I also learned to support women in their quest for Jewish identity, especially when the quest was also spiritual. The possibility of conflict between these two worlds never developed for me, just as I never felt conflicted about being a rabbi and a professor at the same time. I have met many Christian colleagues, and Jews too, who have rejected their religious and spiritual roots in order to join the academy. I never felt the need to do that but I could not figure out how to take spirituality and make it more central to my work.

Taking Theology Seriously The move to Emory University introduced me to serious Christian academics. Men like Jack Boozer and Will Beardslee were not only fine academics, capable of holding their own in any critical intellectual discussion of the sources, they were also seriously committed Christians. Boozer's ethical activity on campus and in the Atlanta community grew out of his Christian commitments. He really believed that the love of Christ included Jews, and African Americans, and women, and even homosexuals—not in a proselytizing way, but in its simple meaning: to love like Christ is to love, period; the rest is commentary. Will Beardslee's commitment to critical New Testament study and to process theology flowed from his understanding of the life of Christ, not just from his reading of the texts. Gene Bianchi, to whom this book is dedicated, has always rooted his concerns with psychology, dreams, aging, and ecology in a persistent Christian spirituality and theology. For all these people, spirituality and academic study went hand in hand. Later, I met other colleagues who also embodied this mixture, and it seemed natural to me though I did not yet see myself this way.

Several years of work with the Presbyterian Church on a document in Christian-Jewish relations opened my eyes for the second time. The document was to be a theological document. As a Jew, I was worried about its political and historical implications. Slowly, it dawned on me that the Presbyterians took theology seriously. They really believed that doctrine made a difference, that what the church taught was important. As a Jew, I could scarcely believe it for, even though I was the one who had been asking "Is that God?," who had written the first textbooks on Jewish mysticism, and who had sent his children to parochial schools, I had learned enough to know that thought alone didn't count; only political stance and action in the social setting counted. Slowly, I realized something: that Jews are instinctively political while Christians are instinctively theological.

But, what if the Presbyterians were right? What if doctrine did count? What if theology was not only an area of *wissenschaftlich* study but also a serious intellectual discipline, a serious spiritual option?

These questions were not new to my Christian colleagues, but they were new to me and, instinct told me, this was the way, this was the path that was intellectual-academic as well as scholarly-spiritual. Of course, I would have to work with Jewish sources and work in a literarily Jewish form, but I could "do theology." So I dug into my own faith and prayer life, and I reopened my study of Abraham Joshua Heschel and Hasidism, and I wrote *God at the Center*. It is a book of *divrei Torah*, of words of Torah-teaching. Each *dvar Torah* contains a problematic biblical text, the spiritual interpretation given by an early Hasidic master, and a theological response by myself. It is a book of spiritual theology, written as a type of commentary to a biblical-Hasidic text and arranged according to the lectionary cycle. It is, thus, Jewish in its form as well as in its content; all those years of studying texts had paid off. It is a beautiful book but it is, alas, theologically naive.

Meanwhile, almost all my great teachers had died. Their deaths freed me from the obligation to be like them, great antiquarians. My father, who was one of the leading rabbis in Conservative Judaism, had also died, freeing me from the obligation to be like him, a builder of institutions within the Jewish community, which I was never very good at anyway. In addition, the great trauma of our century had reared its ugly head. During my entire time in school, the rabbinate, and in Zionist circles, I had heard only one fifty-minute lecture on the shoah. It was a taboo subject, or at least, a very carefully contained topic. Only after the stunning victory of the Six Day War did Jews feel comfortable enough to confront the shoah. The reasons for this are complicated, but the fact remains that I, and I think a large part of the Jewish community as well, came to the shoah after 1967. It became a significant part of my life at Emory University only when, in 1978, Jack Boozer insisted that we teach a course on it. Later, this was followed by the establishment of the Witness to the Holocaust Project by another Christian Emory colleague, Fred Crawford. As the shoah mushroomed as an object of study and commemoration, my own involvement grew. But I did not know how to connect it with Jewish spirituality, with Jewish theology.

A Mid-Life Re-Calling When Jack Boozer died, I felt I owed it to him to do something within the general Atlanta community where my involvements had been peripheral. The Georgia Council on Child Abuse very kindly allowed me to sit in on the monthly supervision sessions for therapists who were doing group work for them. Listening to these very brave people, I heard stories I could not believe -- of physical abuse, of sexual abuse, of drugs, and of ritual abuse -- and I listened to the heart-wrenching struggles of the therapists as they trod the path of helping the abused, lost their way, and returned to the path of good therapy. Then I began to read narratives and studies. I acquired a new vocabulary—splitting, multiple personality disorder, post-traumatic stress syndrome, empowerment, rage—and I learned new rules: never touch without permission, holidays can be a traumatic time, Mother's Day and Father's Day can be a mockery, and middle class status is no protection from abuse. As I pondered this new knowledge, I realized that, since any set of profound insights into the human condition must have an echo in each of us, abuse and the responses to it are a paradigm of human existence, that is, that they are present in most human beings, though in very much diminished strength.

The jump from contemplating abused persons and their lives to an analysis of contemporary Jews in the post-shoah setting was not great, though it was novel. Hypervigilance, hyperalertrness, overreaction, a siege mentality, and an unwillingness to trust—all these characterize the lives of adult survivors of child abuse. They also characterize contemporary Jewish existence after the shoah. We, Jews, are hyperalert when it comes to anti-Semitism and ethnic cleansing. Israelis who react to stone-throwing Palestinian teenagers as if they were nazis are hypervigilant. Neo-orthodox Jews who react to western civilization as if it were the first step in cultural genocide are hyperalert. Still, some kinds of hypervigilance and unwillingness to trust are healthy—we do, after all, have real enemies—just as these reactions are sometimes healthy in adult survivors of child abuse.

Who Is the Abuser?   Then, the question struck me: If we are behaving like abused children in our post-shoah life, who was the abuser? If we are the victims, who is the perpetrator? This is a horrifying question and the more I pondered it, the less I liked it. I confess that, when I came to write the concluding section of Facing the Abusing God: A Theology of Protest, I was physically ill for two days. I just did not want to say what I already knew: that Jews who know about the shoah behave like abused children because we were abused by our Father in heaven, the God of our people. With great effort, I have learned to say this straight out—God is an abusing God—but it is not easy. I am, after all, the same child who asked out of wonder on seeing the cantor, "Is that God?" I am, too, a rabbi, the son of a rabbi, an academic scholar of Judaism, a father, and an active member of the Jewish community.

The Presbyterians were right: theology does count. But to follow the usual theodicies is not productive. Of what, then, can faith consist in the post-shoah, abuse-sensitive world? My answer is: protest. We assert God's living Presence among us in our personal and national lives and we demand that God live up to God's own covenantal promise of justice and fairness. In its most powerful form: God has sinned against us, and God must seek forgiveness from us. This thesis is very Jewish, indeed rather orthodox—until I make suggestions for modifying the liturgy. *Facing the Abusing God: A Theology of Protest* is also very Jewish in form. And, it does "do theology"; it does address the question of faith—reasonable faith after abuse.

Having proposed an answer to the question of God and the shoah, I felt compelled to tackle the question of humanity and the shoah. The issue, as I see it, is twofold: Why did so many people go along with the shoah? And, why did the few who resisted do so? In writing *The Banality of Good and Evil: Moral Lessons from the Shoah and Jewish Tradition*, I realized that perpetrators, bystanders, and rescuers all followed the same few simple social psychological principles. First, they did what was expected of them. If early authorities had modeled and expected altruism, people followed that pattern. If they had modeled and expected close obedience, people behaved accordingly. Second, I noticed that perpetrators, bystanders, and rescuers all responded to social authority in the same mode in which they had experienced childhood discipline. If the latter had been fair and open, people tended to be resistors or rescuers and, if it had been arbitrary, they tended to be bystanders or perpetrators.

All this was fascinating but what did it have to do with theology? To "do theology" with the material, I needed to "do ethics," that is, I needed to draw practical moral and ethical conclusions. My book,

The Banality of Good and Evil: Moral Lessons from the Shoah and Jew-ish Tradition presents many direct and practical moral and ethical teachings drawn from this material. Perhaps the two simplest are: (1) Use whatever authority you have—and we all have some social au-thority—to permit and encourage prosocial behavior. And (2) be fair and open in disciplining those under you. Set the example of respon-sive, reasonable authority. Throughout, my students have sustained me with their interest, concern, and love.

Reflecting Back Theology is the process by which we learn things from life and bring those experiences and insights back into the ac-cumulated tradition. In our day, we study psychology—the inner and social workings of human beings, the expressed and the repressed, the ethically beautiful and the morally ugly—and then we turn again to our traditions and we bring those insights with us, contemplating God and our relationship to God. That is the task of the theologian. It is a task of "inter-pretation," of standing between—between God and the people, and between the tradition and new knowledge. "Do-ing theology" has been my mid-life re-calling. In a strange way, this has really been a "re-turn" to my original query. The sense of wonder has not left me, and life has made me more sober, but the question remains, "Is that God?"

(*David R. Blumenthal is a prolific author and professor of Judaic Studies at Emory University.*)

Chapter Thirteen

Journey Without Maps

William F. Powers

*A priest finds a self in
the classroom*

I take my title from the book which Graham Greene wrote describing his trip through Liberia in 1935. At that time, and even today to some extent, Liberia was an uncharted wilderness. With either great courage or great foolhardiness, that thirty-year-old English convert to Catholicism cut his way through the underbrush, braved disease, endured insects, ate unappetizing food, and lived among people vastly different from any he had ever known. Greene undertook the adventure literally without a map, because none existed. He had to rely on the often faulty information of the people he met along the way. Eventually, he reached his destination, but it had taken him much longer than he had planned and along an unusually circuitous route.

This story is of course a metaphor for my own life. The only difference is that I thought that I had a map when I began my journey. Eventually, although that map proved to be somewhat unreliable, it led me to some fascinating places.

When I was ten years old, Sister Mary Camillus, my fifth grade teacher, noticing that I was squinting in an effort to read what she wrote on the chalk board, used an improvised eye exam to verify her suspicion that I needed glasses. Marching me out of the classroom and down the shiny marble corridor to a window overlooking billboards across the street, she instructed me to read the signs. I could just about make out the largest letters, about the way I could make out the big "E" on a doctor's wall chart. Until this time, I thought that everyone saw things in as blurry a fashion as I did.

Having been advised by Sister of my progressing myopia, my 20-20-vision parents dutifully took me to be fitted for glasses. Instantly, the world was transformed from fog to sunshine, from shadows to light. I can still recapture the delight I experienced when I walked out of the optometrist's office and for the first time saw everything clearly.

Or so it seemed.

Like Sister Camillus and the other Sisters of Charity, the parish priests, my parents, and everyone else I knew, I believed without question all that the one, holy, catholic, and apostolic Church taught. And what the Church taught was that there was no better way for a boy to find happiness and to be of value to others than to become a priest. And so I did.

As I lay face down on the cold cathedral floor on ordination day forty years ago, I thought that I would spend my life as a priest in a pleasant parish such as the one in which I had been raised. Each morning I would button up my cassock, put on my biretta and head over to church for morning Mass. I would visit the sick, bury the dead, and play with the children in the school yard. It was all so clear. But it didn't happen. Right from the beginning my map proved unreliable and my vision unreliable.

My First Work   I was assigned to an inner city parish which was undergoing a rapid racial and ethnic transition. The influx of Puerto Ricans into many Brooklyn parishes had led the bishop to ask for volunteers from our seminary class to study Spanish in Puerto Rico in preparation for an assignment to a parish with an Hispanic population. Somewhat fearful of making a commitment to working with minority group people, I had not volunteered. However, as it turned out, that's exactly where I began. The pastor there let it be known that he expected me as the "junior man" to assume responsibility for the Hispanics who were moving into the neighborhood.

And so a year after ordination, off I went to Puerto Rico where I underwent the intensive language and cultural program which I had avoided the previous year. I, who had seldom ventured far from my

New York City birthplace, was now traveling on weekends to Puerto Rican rural parishes where I was expected to help the local clergy. One little boy upon exiting my confessional said to his friend, "The priest was talking to me in English." So much for my Spanish! In any case, I returned to Brooklyn as the "Spanish priest" and at once inaugurated a Sunday mass in that language, sweating over the preparation of my homily and reluctant to admit that as often as not I didn't really understand what people said to me. Nevertheless, week by week the congregation grew and with it my confidence. I found myself associated with an amazingly loving community of highly committed, if educationally deficient, Christians. The choir was energetic and the 100 men and women who underwent that intensive evangelization experience called a "Cursillo" provided a leaven in the neighborhood, which brought scores of lapsed Catholics back to the church. Nearly every week I was validating the marriages of couples who had married civilly and baptizing the older children of parents who now felt connected to something vital. Though reared in a straight-laced Irish neighborhood, I fell in love with the Puerto Ricans who had embraced me as their "Padre Hispano."

Even before the Vatican Council convened in 1963, I was well on the way to being a much freer and more flexible human being than I had anticipated. The self that was emerging surprised even me. And the council proceedings really energized us young priests working in the inner city. Our elderly pastors, unprepared for the tidal wave of change which swept away their secure world, abdicated control to the Sixties Generation of clerical young Turks. We turned the altars around and the parishes upside down.

But we were being transformed intellectually and spiritually as well. In the seminary we had been given to believe that we had learned everything we needed to know as priests. If this had been true in the pre-conciliar period, it certainly was no longer true in the mid-sixties. Accordingly, like many of my contemporaries, at my own expense I enrolled in graduate school, undertaking the study of sociology at St. John's University.

Changing Times But sociology was happening at home too. My Bedford-Stuyvesant parish was a major caldron of unrest during the Civil Rights movement and a primary battleground in the War on

Poverty. As little as I understood of the Latino culture, I understood even less about the social and political structure of our country in general. I had lived my life in the security of the Catholic ghetto, but now the larger world was demanding my attention. Soon all the ambiguities of the Vietnam War were added to the mix as we broadened our understanding of priesthood—even if, in our zeal, we may have gone too far in preaching our political views from the pulpit. We were intoxicated with the prospect of playing a role in shaping the church and the world. In the thrill of "making a difference," my truer self was emerging.

But our spiritual lives suffered in the excitement of the period. We spent more time holding meetings and going to rallies than on our knees. The Divine Office was judged irrelevant and the rosary and benediction of the Blessed Sacrament obsolete. For a time, only smugness and excessive self-confidence replaced them. The noise of change made it difficult to hear the voice of God.

Through my academic sociological studies, I took on a more scientific way of looking at reality. A priest with whom I lived disapproved of my going to school, arguing that sociology was communism and that it would endanger my faith. It turned out that he was correct: it was religiously dangerous. In any case, just as my several periods of study in Puerto Rico contributed to my "adult education," so also did the years I spent studying sociology. In combination with the decrees coming forth from the Vatican council, my education was fashioning in me a very different and unexpected self. There were fewer absolutes in my life, more questions, more experimentation.

One of the experiments was falling in love. In a 1967 article in *America*, Eugene Kennedy described "the third way," a combination of celibacy and a deep man-woman relationship. "Latent heterosexuality" was bursting forth all over the vowed world. We were being taught that every "I" needed a "thou," and that maturity could not be attained without openness to the opposite sex. My relationship with one of the sisters in the parish school developed slowly but became progressively more intense. Neither of us was thinking of leaving the celibate life and our time together was discreet and chaste. It continued for a number of years, even as she moved on to other assignments, including Puerto Rico. There, I visited her on several occasions for what turned out to be romantic encounters on a tropical isle. Photographs show her in a white habit and me in black trousers and sport shirt. The deep love we felt for each other (ever so celibate) might be faulted as unhealthy repression, but it seemed right then and still seems right today. She remains a committed Religious. Part of her ministry and achievement as a young sister was to show a young priest that he was lovable.

So nine years into my priesthood, the parish Spanish program was on a firm footing, and I had multiple involvements in community development projects. I had earned an M.A. and was on my way to a Ph.D. in sociology. Also, I was teaching as an adjunct faculty member in the Theology Department at St. John's University. Everything seemed perfect. Yet under the surface there was a restlessness. The work of parish priest no longer seemed challenging. At one time, I had pictured myself as a sort of Cure of Ars working quietly in the same parish for decades, baptizing children, and then in time marrying them and baptizing their children. But this image of priesthood now felt hopelessly out of date. It wasn't going to happen.

Thinking that perhaps my problem was that I had been too long in the inner city, I requested a transfer and was assigned to an affluent area at the other end of the diocese. There I quickly antagonized traditionalists but won the friendship of more liberal Catholics, some of whom have remained friends to this day. However, I soon realized that the problem was not my assignment; the problem was that I no longer wanted to be a member of the celibate clergy. I looked at the other priests at the dinner table and knew that I didn't want to grow old with them. Something within me was pushing me out the rectory door.

And so a stage in life ended and another began. There was much about the work of the priest which I loved, including saying mass and preaching. But Catholic priesthood is not a job which one can perform and then go home. For priests there is no "home," no separation between work and self. I needed that separation, and I needed a partner.

Toward Teaching Initially, I had no thought of teaching in college. My inner city experience, academic degree, and knowledge of Spanish qualified me for a position with the New York City antipoverty

program. Idealistically, I believed that working in the central administration of the agency would enable me to help the poor. However,
even though I worked directly with one of the assistant commission-
ers and often attended top level meetings, I spent most of my time
filling out forms required for funding by Washington. Within months,
I knew that I was in the wrong place and turned my thoughts in the
direction of college teaching.

In the meanwhile, I had rented an apartment, and for the first
time in my life was responsible for my own meals, laundry, and house-
keeping. Shedding the clerical persona and becoming a "regular man"
was an intoxicating experience. Even more central to the shaping of
my new identity was meeting and falling in love with the woman
who would become my wife. She was a bright and beautiful academic, a former nun, and bursting with joy and energy. Our months
of courting and finally our marriage drew me powerfully into my
truest self. She seemed to be having the same experience. Although I
didn't know what would come next in my work life, it was spring
again. If there was no map, at least there was the adventure.

Fortunately, the uncertainty soon ended. What would be the
framework for my work life for the next three decades began with a
notice pinned on our apartment door. One day, arriving home from
the antipoverty agency, I found that my wife had posted on the door:
"Welcome home, Assistant Professor Powers." Too excited to wait,
she had opened the letter from Suffolk Community College on Long
Island which offered me a position in the Sociology Department.

And so, after a lengthy commitment to urban problems, I now
joined the hundreds of thousands of men and women who were trans-
forming once-rural areas into comfortable middle class suburban communities. Although these suburbs attempted to insulate themselves
from "The City," (which had become synonymous with crime, con-
gestion, and noise), I told myself that my mission was to bring to my
students a concern for the less fortunate and a more positive appreciation of urban life. Perhaps symptomatic of the challenge I faced
was that the first course which I taught, American Ethnic Groups,
designed specifically to broaden awareness of the increasing diversity
which characterized America, was eventually dropped from the department offerings due to chronic lack of enrollment. The ground
was moving beneath my feet.

Despite such difficulties, teaching was very satisfying. I remember a colleague saying that he loved the job so much that he would do it even if they didn't pay him. I felt the same way. It was not unlike the early years of working with Puerto Ricans in Brooklyn. Now my congregation was not Catholic but public school students attending a community college. I had never attended a public school or heard of community colleges. Once again, I felt thrown into a different cultural world, that of the academically marginal suburban adolescent. This time I did not have to learn Spanish but rather the much more difficult language of the younger generation. For a time I believed that I was making some headway, preaching the scientific method from my secular pulpit and exhorting students to think and to write more clearly.

For a number of years I couldn't get enough of the classroom. I taught summer sessions and night classes, not only earning more money for a growing family and larger house, but finding sociological ideas fascinating and taking delight in challenging conservative students with the Marxist perspective on social issues. My main course was Marriage and the Family, which provided a forum for exploring such real world issues as abortion, cohabitation, and divorce. In a sense, I was doing substantially more "premarital counseling" than I ever did as a member of the clergy.

Although canonically marginal to the institutional church, my wife and I attended Mass faithfully, participating actively in the vital campus parish at a nearby university. Here our children received their first Communion and were confirmed. (In an earlier more rebellious phase of identity seeking, I had baptized the children myself in home liturgies in which many of our friends from the past participated.) For twenty years, aided by a deeply spiritual yet highly intellectual priest friend, the various dimensions of our lives stayed in harmony.

New Directions However, imperceptibly at first, teaching was becoming less stimulating. In a parallel to my experience as a priest, I thought that a change in what I was teaching would revitalize me. Therefore, I developed new courses, including one on the baby boom generation, and earned additional graduate credits in order to teach cultural anthropology and psychology. But just as a transfer to the suburban parish didn't really help me years before, the new subject matter now did not still my restlessness. It was clear that once again life was prompting me to turn in a new direction.

But what was I to do? Help came in the form of that most wonderful of all academic perquisites, the sabbatical. Since my wife was teaching college also, she was able to get a leave or a sabbatical herself as over the course of our careers we took three full years away from our Long Island academic commitments. The first was spent in Texas, where I conducted research for a church-related volunteer agency; the second was in St. Louis where I wrote a book on priesthood; the third was in North Carolina where, with diocesan encouragement, I researched the history of the church in that state. A neglected side of myself was emerging, that side which found the private world of research and writing more satisfying than the more public forum of the classroom.

In his book on his journey through Liberia, Graham Greene relates an encounter with a German who was studying the cultures of the region. Greene said of the man, "teaching tired him as much as learning invigorated him." This is what I was discovering about myself. Community colleges as a rule stress teaching over research. In fact, so little importance is given to research that job candidates with strong research interests are likely to be rejected. The reasoning is that they would not be content devoting most of their energies to teaching. Although I had a doctorate for which I had conducted research in social gerontology, basically I accepted the college's priorities and, aside from occasionally reading papers at conferences, for many years conducted very little research and wrote almost nothing.

And so the focus of my work shifted from the classroom to the word processor, from interaction with students to the silence of my own mind. To some extent, I was returning to the academic equivalent of the dark seminary chapel where at times something wonderful would happen. The Spirit spoke and a page of the book of life was turned and the smell of incense delighted the soul. At other times, there was only the dolorous ticking of the clock, the aching muscles, and the taste of fatigue. Now, decades later, as I struggled to write, the advice of a long deceased seminary spiritual director echoed in my mind. When I would complain about the aridity, he would reply patiently: Just stay there, put in the time, trust.

That clock continues to tick today, of course. The shadows lengthen. My retirement from teaching signals yet another transition. What lies ahead seems strangely like a return to where I began. The first paper I ever had published was written while I was in the seminary. The church history professor who had encouraged me to write guided me to the Jesuit Relations, dusty tomes buried in the dark recesses of the attic where books which no one ever used were stored. I was alone up there with my thoughts and my dreams, taking notes about people long dead. Now, more than forty years later, I find myself in the dusty archives of the Raleigh, North Carolina, diocese, carefully turning the pages of the yellowing diary of its first bishop.

If there is any way to sum up my work life and relate it to who I am, it might be in terms of the verse from John's Gospel: The Word was made flesh and lived among us. Words have been my work. First in the pulpit and the confessional, then in the classroom and office, and later in the library and archives, I have attempted to bring words to life, to give them flesh. As the life of Jesus demonstrates, such work can be both human and divine. Words link us with one another and with God; words skim across the surface of our hearts and dive to the depths of our souls and live among us. Words can hurt, and words can heal. They are the vehicles through which life is transmitted across space and time. Words to a writer are the song of birds awakening us in the morning and accompanying us as we fall asleep at night.

At times, when I look out the window, the signs along the road look crisp and clear, as they did when a child put on his first pair of eyeglasses many years ago. At other times the words are blurred, indecipherable. I squint and strain to make out the message. But there is no fear. Firm, reassuring hands, human and divine, touch my shoulder. I've become my *self*, and know I am cherished as such.

(*William F. Powers is an author, a former college professor, and a retired Roman Catholic priest. He is the author of* Free Priests, Loyola University Press, 1992, *and* Alive and Well, Rutledge Books, 1996.)

Intermezzo IV

Be your note

God picks up the reed-flute world, and blows.
Each note is a need
    but coming through one of us:
    a passion, a longing-pain.
Remember the lips
    where the wind-breath began
    and let your note be clear.
Try not to let it end.
Be your note.

I'll show you how it becomes its full self:
    go up on the roof at night
    in this city of the soul.
Let everyone climb on their roofs.
Then sing out your notes!
Sing loud! Sing loud!

Jelaluddin Rumi

Chapter Fourteen

WHAT I DO IS ME

John A. Coleman

*The teacher stretches
beyond teaching*

The conceit of Hirokozu Kore-Eda's arresting Japanese-language film *After Life* builds upon a narrative about a group of newly arrived, recently dead, souls who sojourn a week at an interim testing-facility in the mountains. Their task is to recall and, then, deliberately choose one singular memory which—and it alone!—they will subsequently experience eternally. If they fail to fasten on or select a given memory, after a week's time, they will be doomed to lag behind in a kind of purgatory of service-attendance to the next generation of arriving souls, who will undergo their own trial of memory.

Some of the characters in the film simply refuse to choose among their myriad memories in a defiant: 'Let all the thousand flowers bloom!' Some select trivial and banal amusements. Some only hold horrid recollections they do not want as eternal keep-sakes. Some see their past lives as insipid. Others recall, with fondness, scenes of tender affection and sensual vibrancy. But the task set before them all remains: they will spend all eternity with one singular thing they have done which they choose to remember.

I rehearse this humane film as I am faced with an analogous task for this book. From what I do or have done, what do I select as a token of who I am ? " What I do is me"—the theme of this volume—

contains much ambiguity. Am I determined or has my identity been entirely or primarily shaped by what I have done ? Few of us surmise, with the Latin poet Horace, that we have built, in our work, a monument more lasting than bronze! My Christian resonance with salvation by grace not works makes such a thought repugnant. So, I mightily resist equating myself with my work in hopes that my essential being might just possibly be larger and more interesting than my paltry actions. Yet to take this hopeful tack risks trivializing our work as a vocation, a calling to become a kind of agent, a craft-testing of our mettle, a forging of the kind of person we have become.

Concomitantly, I am sorely tempted to reverse the verbs to read: What I am, I do. For the ancient scholastic philosophers, the order runs thus: agere sequitur esse—what I do flows from the kind of person I am. I also find this formulation congenial since I think perduring character feeds into, as much as it flows out from, our work. Perhaps, though, this is to assume a too static, essentialist, and non-developmental view of the person. It is to forget—as Simone Weil once trenchantly put it—how our work actually profoundly bores into us to stamp us and leave a permanent mark, how it enters even our bodies (there is a teacher's posture, a preacher's voice, a ditch-digger's hands). In truth, through our work we gradually and inevitably become what we do. I have chosen , then, three terms to sum up who I am from the work I have done: Jesuit, sociologist, teacher. For each, I want to link the work with a spirituality ingredient in it.

***

Jesuit   I joined the Jesuits at age seventeen, forty-five years ago. What it means for me to be a Jesuit today is quite different—surely both more enriched and more down to earth—than what it meant to me then. Ideally, at least, Jesuits see themselves as a company of true friends in the Lord, a celibate and international brotherhood engaged in a great variety of disparate works which look—in an old-fashioned phrase—primarily to 'helping souls'. Over the years, Jesuits have been many things: diplomats, scholars, teachers, social workers, playwrights, musicians, painters, astonomers, pastors, spiritual directors, fund raisers, journalists, bush missionaries. At root, however, the many ministries of the Jesuits coalesce in various forms of preaching broadly understood. Teaching, spiritual direction, even ' spiritual conversation' are all seen as variants of this primary ministry of the word. And as the Company of Jesus, what Jesuits hope to preach and embody in their lives is the gospel message of Jesus.

A hermeneutic of the Jesuits as a lived spiritual tradition would be difficult to mount with honesty, integrity and justice to its many facets and shortcomings. The Jesuits represent a complicated tradition and, like all traditions, the Jesuits also have their shadow side, historic failures and blind spots. It is fitting, of course, that one who is still a practicing Jesuit contribute to a festschrift for Gene Bianchi because Bianchi spent twenty-odd years as a Jesuit and has recently been working on a study of the religious sensibilities of contemporary American Jesuits and former Jesuits. Undoubtedly, that experience has stamped Gene's spirituality with perduring elements from his Jesuit past. I share Gene's desire to find out empirically how contemporary Jesuits actually see their lives of community, prayer, obedience, celibacy, life-style and apostolic ministry. I suspect that Gene and I diverge very broadly, however, in our analysis of that data and our prescriptions for a reformulation of the Jesuit tradition. While I am very open and enthusiastic about a genuine enrichment of that tradition through dialogue with world religions and see that dialogue as an integral part of my Jesuit vocation, I think I am less likely than Gene is to simply substitute Buddhist or humanist concepts or practice for Christian ones. I am also an opponent of married Jesuits (which is something quite different from my position on clerical celibacy for diocesan priests). Not all Jesuits are priests. Most entered the Jesuits to be part of a religious brotherhood rather than specifically to be priests. Jesuit celibacy is not at all directly linked to priesthood.

I know I did not enter the Jesuits to be a priest. Priesthood was an afterthought and a kind of natural, if lovely, after-effect. But I could contentedly be a Jesuit brother, if I could still write, teach and engage in the broad ministry of the word. As a thought experiment, I have often said that, if the Jesuits were suppressed again by one of the popes, I would not feel bound to remain a priest but I would look for some analogous celibate, apostolic religious brotherhood to join. Celibacy for me—which has been at many times a true struggle—is a spiritual attempt to be more available to the Lord, to my community and to apostolic service. Not that I have very much to boast about in terms of my empirical behavior on this score but only that the ideal seems to me vital and lovely for those who truly choose and experience it as freeing. I do not think it is a chimera or likely destructive for me.

Again, while I want the Jesuits to learn new ways to cooperate and closely collaborate with non-Jesuit co-workers, I would not simply merge the existing form of the Jesuits with a new amalgamation of third-order Jesuits which mixes and matches married, Christian and non-Christian, elements in one unified organization. I am not terribly impressed by the experiments of the Grail or the former Immaculate Heart Community in Los Angeles in going down that path. The sociologist in me, for one, distrusts the identity dilution in such a move. I tend to think that, even if new forms of religious constellation are truly needed in the Roman Catholic Church to supplement earlier, classical forms of religious life around the three vows, it is unlikely that the older forms are flexible enough to become carriers of the new. Older forms need, to be sure, reform and some reformulation to allow them to adapt to new times and situations. But the major carrier groups of new religious organization for the twenty-first century will arise afresh, as they did in the nineteenth and earlier in the sixteenth centuries. A charism, once institutionalized, has adaptability, but only limited flexibility to embrace radically new forms. It is stuck, willy-nilly, with the characteristic limits and contours of its historic identity. While I do not think the Jesuits are, by any long shot, fossils, they will continue on, if they do, with much continuity of identity. As sociologists of religion note, no one religious form can adapt to all niches.

Both Bianchi and I desire the reform of the Jesuits and the reform of the Catholic Church and have worked for those ends. I suspect that the shape of the reform we each envision for both is quite different. My own reform agenda, for the church, still flows from the essential spirit of Vatican II which has not yet been institutionalized and, for the Jesuits, from General Congregation 34 which has also not yet been institutionalized. But this is not the place for an extended dialogue comparing how a still-insider Jesuit who prizes institutions sees the group he remains committed to, as opposed to a former Jesuit's loving critique of the group he left and yet remains deeply interested in.

I can not now imagine myself not being a Jesuit. I suppose I became over time what I have worked at doing for forty-five years. For me (of course, other Jesuits would appropriate the tradition differently), the Jesuit spirituality brings together a unique blend of four disparate elements:

(1) **A love for and dedication to the intellectual life** From their beginnings, the Jesuits have been involved with research and universities. The integrity of learning must be respected and never simply subordinated to the institutional interests or purposes of the church or even some noble pastoral purpose. The mind, in this view, has some real access to the glory of God in its multiple splendors. The Jesuits have sustained a long tradition of serious scholarship in many fields and not just in theology, in the belief that the Glory of God arises out of the human person fully alive and knowledgeable. God and humans are neither equals nor competitors. God desires that the human become fully a knower and seeker after knowledge. I could never be content with a work which did not include study and research and growth in knowledge.

(2) **A commitment to a deep and vibrant spiritual life** Jesuits follow the spiritual wisdom and practices of St. Ignatius as found in his famous Spiritual Exercises. Key here is not only to appropriate the mind and spirit of Jesus in the gospels and his work to bring about God's kingdom of justice, but a ' finding of God in all things'. This central contemplation of the Ignatian Exercises feeds into an intellectual and spiritual openness which does not preclude God's action anywhere or determine, in advance, how God will or must be present. I have always loved a very traditional Jesuit director of Exercises who actually saw—to his great surprise—that his directee was being led by God to abandon Catholicism to return to her mother's faith of Judaism. He credited that movement as from the Spirit. To be sure, spirituality for the Jesuit (and for this Jesuit) is informed by definite practices such as daily prayer, contemplation, examination of consciousness, a discernment of motions and spirits of the psyche, forms

of asceticism, spiritual reflection and retreat. But spirituality is not just a piety unrelated to the intellect. Nor is it opposed to genuine humanism. It is mainly to help us become more free, so God's action and purposes can more influence us. The Jesuit spirituality I try to embody contains a vector, somehow, to bring heart and mind, emotions and intellect in conformity and concert (or, at the minimum, in conversation). It calls me to try to love and enact whatever is good in God's purposes and creation, whatever gives fuller life to the human and glory to God.

(3) **A Care for justice** In recent years, the Jesuits have referred to their charism as one of 'the faith that does justice.' With a characteristic lack of humility, the Jesuits, of course, rarely admit that this new emphasis comes to them as a gift from the wider church (especially in third world settings) with its new stress on an option for the poor. But the Jesuits now insist that all Jesuit works—intellectual, social, pastoral—must look to and embody a care for justice. These three elements overlap. Characteristically, a Jesuit concern for justice will link up with intellectual social analysis and a spirituality to give work for social justice a depth and staying power. If Jesuit intellectual endeavors also envision the care for societal justice, this should lead to a new sense of Jesuits as a 'company of critics,' public intellectuals concerned also for the truth and integrity of just social structures in church and society. A Jesuit intellectual will see his love of learning as a sub-species of spirituality, the love of God. Spirituality, on its part, will not just concern itself with some 'interior garden' but with care for justice. I have always been a sucker whenever I see these three components of respect for the integrity of intellectual life, spirituality and a concern for justice come together, whether I find it among Jesuits or anyone else.

(4) **Service to the Church** The Jesuits were founded to help reform the Catholic Church (which is ever in need of reform) in the period of the Counter-Reformation. Early on, the first Ignatian documents insisted on Jesuits 'having a proper attitude of service in the church', in what was called *sentire cum ecclesia*—taking on one's root sensibilities in and through and with the church. This remains core to my own spirituality. As the recent document of the Jesuit Congregation 34 puts this, this care for ecclesial life will recognize that ecumenism

is an authentic new way of being a Catholic Christian. It will acknowledge, as well, the distinctive and inalienable ecclesial role of the laity in the life of the church. It will know that "the more public service of scholarly research, teaching, speaking, writing are intellectual tasks that require freedom, openness and courage in the objective service of the truth." It will see that Jesuit service to the church "can also oblige us to engage in constructive criticism, based on prayerful discernment." It will define the church as a koinonia of local churches and recover an ecclesiology of collegial co-responsibility.

One implication of this concern for service to the church is that, for the Jesuit, the intellectual life entails a responsibility not only to academia and its legitimate and exacting standards but also to the church. As a Christian intellectual, as David Tracy has argued, the Jesuit intellectual will try to serve and respond to three distinct, yet related, publics: academia, society and the church.

Much of the above must seem a heavily idealized portrait, but my own intellectual work has tried to touch all four of these elements. Over the years I have regularly taught, every year, courses and workshops on Catholic social teaching and theories of justice and have written on these themes. I have supplemented this intellectual work on justice with some active memberships in social justice movements such as Amnesty International and Bread for the World. More humbly, I tutor weekly a group of undocumented Hispanics in survival English. This contact, in turn, forces me to confront unjust immigration laws, unfair labor practices and fear of the stranger in our society.

For twenty-three years I served as a faculty member in an academic setting, The Graduate Theological Union in Berkeley, which trained ministers—in an ecumenical, even inter-religious, setting— for service to the churches. The doctoral program I taught in was an inter-disciplinary effort to join sociology and social ethics together. It represents a joint effort with the sociology department at the University of California. I have always regularly preached in Catholic and ecumenical liturgies (the ministry of the word being, for me, of primacy). I have both written on spirituality and practiced (as recipient and giver) spiritual direction on a regular basis. I direct at least one retreat every year, for the last few years with Roman Catholic bishops. I have tried to stay abreast and contribute in a scholarly way to the academic discipline of sociology, especially the sub-branch of sociology of religion where I hold active memberships in the Association for the Sociology of Religion and the Society for the Scientific Study of Religion. I have worked with bishops, Catholic Conferences at the state and national levels, and ecclesial groups to draft policy statements and pastoral documents.

Not that I have necessarily done any of these things very well. But these four elements—the integrity of the intellectual life, a commitment to spirituality, a care for justice and service to the church—have served me and I want them to continue to operate as bench-marks for deciding which invitations to accept and what to research and write. In that sense, I see my work as flowing as much from "What I am" as a Jesuit as from what I do.

***

Sociologist At age seventeen when I entered the Jesuits, I also knew I wanted to study sociology. I had been mainly inspired to enter the Jesuits by a Jesuit scholastic, John Clark, who taught me in senior year of high school a semester of sociology and a semester of economics. John was and is more an economist than a sociologist. He has always told me that I got it wrong and I should have become an economist. But having had to read John Maynard Keynes' famous treatise A General Theory of Employment, Interest and Money for Clark's class, economics always seemed to me to have aptly earned its infamous sobriquet as the dismal science. I can also never imagine myself as, in some real sense, not a sociologist. In the early years, I was drawn to sociology as an ameliorative science to address urgent social problems such as American racism and the problem of workers. My father was a union organizer and his influence made me want to know what impeded American society from achieving more just social arrangements. It also led me to an interest in differential power in social settings.

The Jesuits were never very enamored of me becoming a sociologist. When I was in what the Jesuits called in those days, the juniorate, where we majored in classical Latin and Greek literature, they tried to detour me into the study of classics. As an antidote, I read all of

Pitirim Sorokin's work during siestas. When I went to study philosophy at St. Louis, the Jesuits there tried to entice me to major in philosophy. During that period, I found (strange as it may now sound) solace in reading through the collected work of Talcott Parsons and—less strange—taking courses from the brilliant Jesuit family sociologist, John Thomas.

I went to study for my doctorate in sociology at the University of California, Berkeley. At that time, Berkeley was absolutely unparalleled anywhere in the world (before or since since Berkeley no longer has the sociology of religion resources it then had) in sociology of religion. I was drawn to that sub-specialty mainly because it overlapped with my Jesuit commitments. I was initially attracted to Berkeley to work with Charles Glock who did masterful survey research studies on religion. I did study with him and did research for a time on his Christian belief and anti-Semitism studies.

But Robert Bellah became the mentor at Berkeley who I was most ready for. He combined in his person and intellectual work that triad I have lifted up earlier as part of the tradition of Jesuit spirituality: a love for and dedication to the intellectual life; a commitment to a deep and vibrant spiritual life and a care for justice. From him I learned to prize a hermeneutic understanding of sociology and the sense that sociology was concerned not just—positivistically—with what exists and how it works but with underlying images of social pathology and the good society. Bellah also showed me that sociology of religion should not be narrowly construed as some mere sub-discipline of the field but as central to the understanding of social structures. If every sociology, as Bellah once put it, implies a theology (often poorly thematized), every theology also implies a sociology (often wrong-headed). Over the years, I have been drawn to write and speak on the relation of theology and sociology.

But if Bellah set an indispensable intellectual style and ethos to my understanding of the social sciences (broadly historical and comparative and using rich literary and philosophic resources), another teacher at Berkeley, Ivan Vallier, set a more precise research agenda. Vallier had written one masterful book entitled Catholicism, Social Change and Modernization in Latin America which I devoured and outlined and underlined and studied over and over. I also read every article he ever wrote in obscure European journals such as Social Compass and Revues des Recherches de Sciences Religiouse on, e.g., the diocese as a strategic unit of analysis and the church as a transnational actor. At that time, I did not feel that Bellah was sufficiently structuralist in his imagination, that he stressed culture too much as an overly inde-pendent variable and that—as in his famous article on religious evo-lution—he tended to think of modern Catholicism as essentially a survivor pre-modern form in modern societies. I thought that posi-tion foolish (and Bellah has since changed his mind on this point) and found a very different account in Vallier whose structural imagi-nation was fecund and who knew which structural variables to lift up in comparative studies of Catholic systems. Vallier's work was an unmistakable background for my book, *The Evolution of Dutch Ca-tholicism* and also (perhaps not so obvious to the reader) in my book, *An American Strategic Theology.*

Recent sociological work I have been doing on paradenominational groups and on Catholic Charities U.S.A. continue this Vallier influ-ence. My major concerns in sociology of religion are, broadly, the structural pre-conditions for religion having influence on its host societies. I suspect that any future sociological work I do will con-tinue that essentially Weberian question. While one doesn't usually associate sociology with spirituality (more often sociology is linked to the corroding acids of modernity), for me the sociological imagi-nation helps to situate what are the real concrete possibilities for ac-tion to change or have leverage on the structures of society. It is a chastening ascesis in the intellectual order, both in its bracing realism (what *is* and stubbornly effects our fondest hopes and actions) and in its utopian imagination (alternative prospects for a good, just and humane society and their structural prerequisites). Sociology helps us to discover the real obstacles and vehicles for justice. In something akin to an exercise of humility, the sociological imagination also forces us to inspect subtle and unanticipated consequences of social inter-ventions. At any rate, most of my writing and teaching in sociology seems perfectly justified under the Ignatian principle that it is always better to know and discern the various movements in life and society than simply to react blindly to them. And over the years, I persistently teach courses in sociology of religion and the sociology of American Catholicism.

Even when I teach courses which are not technically 'sociology,' e.g., seminars I regularly teach on theories of justice or on Catholic social teaching, I tend to approach these topics from a distinctively sociological perspective. Thus, I am more interested in the social movements which gave rise to the Catholic social teaching than to the encyclicals or pastoral letters as wordy documents. I am more concerned with the preconditions for implementing the vision of Catholic social teaching and the institutions needed for such implementation than in the ethical principles (as abstract norms) or theology which undergirds the social teaching. At its best, I see no reason why sociology can not serve as a congenial meeting ground for my proposed triad: dedication to the intellectual life; a commitment to a deep and vibrant life of spiritual meaning and a care for justice.

***

Teacher I found some very congenial language which resonates with my own long and varied experience as a teacher in a book I recently read by the Quaker sociologist and educator, Parker Palmer, *The Courage to Teach*. Its sub-title, "Exploring the Inner Landscape of a Teacher's Life," points to essential elements of spirituality in the teacher's vocation. As with the terms, Jesuit and sociologist, I also can not imagine myself ever not being a teacher. I have been doing it, in some form, since I was a high school student, teaching catechetics to grade school students. And when I retire, I expect to use teaching skills as a volunteer.

With Palmer, I believe that the teacher brings to any learning situation not just the question of what is to be taught or how it is to be taught but the *who* question—who is the teacher and his or her qualities of identity and integrity? Who are the students ? Even as teachers we must regularly face our own shadows and limits, wounds and fears and that is a spiritual task. Our failures (and successes) as teachers lie less in techniques than in the inner quality of our character, of caring and communicating. In a profound sense, every form of authentic teaching embraces, beyond essential skills, a concern for virtue. It is a spiritual task.

A good teacher (who remains, forever, always also a learner) and good educational processes contain built-in elements connected with the spiritual traditions: moments of solitude and silence, meditative reading practices, a spirituality of care for the whole student. As Palmer well notes: "Teaching is a daily exercise in vulnerability. I need not reveal personal secrets to feel naked in front of a class. I need only parse a sentence or work a proof on the board while my students doze off or pass notes. No matter how technical my subject may be, the things I teach are things I care about—and what I care about helps define my selfhood."

Teachers who live disconnected lives are not good teachers. Teachers who separate head from heart, facts from feelings, theory from practice, teaching from learning are also not good teachers. Teaching involves always a kind of mentoring to help students find their own inner teacher. The vocation of teaching touches at crucial points into classic spirituality. Palmer suggests we use a middle term between 'teacher-centered' and 'student-centered' teaching. He refers to 'subject-centered' education where the great and true and beautiful things—intrinsic goods which can not be just manipulated—grip both teachers and students and provide an exacting standard for each of their behaviors.

Under the spell of great things (i.e., subjects worthy of a life's pursuit of knowledge), we practice honesty, not only because we owe it to one another, but because to lie about what we have seen or discovered would be to betray the truth of great things. We experience humility, not because we have experienced failures (which we have and we hope to learn from them) but because humility is the only appropriate lens through which great things can be seen—and once we have seen them, humility is the only posture possible. We become free men and women through education, not because we have privileged information as an elite of learning, but because despotisms, in whatever form, can be overcome only by invoking the grace of great things: truth, freedom, authenticity, community, justice. Inasmuch as education represents a true conversation between students and teachers about great things, it demands practices of listening, of presuming good-will and desires for growth and authenticity among the interlocutors, of respect and care. The matrix of good teaching and learning is a kind of bond of love. So, teaching is a profoundly spiritual practice, as the great teachers from the Buddha to Jesus to Gandhi have always known.

I grew up in a family where one was not expected to have a properly intellectual autobiography. And if, perchance, you had one, you might decently keep it to yourself! I also was a very close friend of the distinguished sociologist of religion, Elizabeth Nottingham who taught, for many years, a course on constructing one's autobiography at the Starr King School for the Ministry in Berkeley. Elizabeth, herself, wrote a lively autobiography when she was turning eighty. Elizabeth tutored me, however, to a systematic suspicion of autobiographers who, frequently, are deluded or evoke self-serving accounts. Often the biographer better understands the deepest motives of the subject than the autobiographer does.

So, I am aware of the pitfalls in this autobiographical exercise about my work and spirituality. I remember the many times I have deviated, in practice, from my operative ideals as a Jesuit, sociologist and teacher. I recoil, in horror, when I rehearse the times I was more a fear-ridden teacher who turned the classroom into a pedagogical prison, than a mentor. There are enough bad memories under each of the rubrics of Jesuit, sociologist and teacher which I would shudder to retain as eternal keep-sakes. I feel shoddy about some sociological work which remained too conceptual and conjectural. Yet, when I examine—as a kind of mental experiment—the task set before the souls in Kore-Eda's film, *After Life*, I feel confident that some of my typical memories would be pleasant eternal companions. Because I still feel so incomplete in each of the roles and what I have done under their rubrics I feel my spiritual journey through work may only now just be beginning.

(John A. Coleman, S.J., is a prolific author and editor, and is Casassa Professor in Social Values at Loyola Marymount University, Los Angeles, California.)

Chapter Fifteen

DREAMING UP A SELF

William Cleary

*An inventor invents
a self*

In 1976 when you stepped up into Hopkins Bookshop, you
found yourself in a tunnel-shaped space colored with earthen
shades of orange and green, and the prevailing smell of gar-
lic—which came from the sub shop next door linked to us by
a common basement, a dank stone-edged cave where we had
our office. One October evening a dreamy-eyed visitor to a poetry
reading disappeared down that stairs, and, never seen to come back
up, she became a myth. My guess was she had met the ghost of the
great Jesuit poet, Gerard Manley Hopkins, (who had died in 1889
and whom we named the store after) and together, ghost and sylph,
they help kingfisher poets catch fire worldwide.

The upstairs was bright though, and a 40-foot mural outside
carried our orange and green motif down the side-street alley. The
mural depicted ten famous quotations from Hopkins laid out word
after word along a waterfront image at your feet, decorating the nearby
shore, edging the surface of a placid Lake Champlain, with some
higher-up quotations riding up and down distant Adirondacks, and
encircling stylized trees, clouds and an upside down rainbow, all orange and sun-bathed. Other Hopkins quotations sang from odd places
on the inside store walls, and in our bathroom over the sink it said:
"Wildness and wet, wildness and wet, long live the woods and the
wilderness yet." It was Hopkins-land, a place styled after the thought
and religious ideals of the Victorian poet who to this day captivates
my admiration.

You would have seen all this in Burlington, Vermont, the little state's most bustling city, a bookstore located right across from City Hall, and situated on the last block of a 4-block Main Street leading up to a white colonial church with "1816" high on its red brick clock tower.

On a good day our greeting card displays would be spinning, a rabbi would be browsing among our Jewish books in the window, two nuns from one of the nearby Catholic colleges would be asking for new titles by Schillebeeckx and Rahner, while my wife (a part-time campus minister at the University of Vermont, just up the hill) would be activating the clumsy ching of our ancient brass cash register, and Yours Truly would be sitting on the steps leading up to our children's section reading the *Narnia Tales* to two pre-school children who clearly resembled both me *and* the check-out lady.

If the poet Hopkins is on target when he opines that "every mortal thing deals out that being indoors dwells, selves, goes itself, proclaiming 'what I do is me,' "this whole bookstore scene is a snapshot of myself at age fifty. On my face one might read the intensity lines of one who had been a Jesuit for twenty two years, who married at forty three and had become the father of two challenging sons. My bride had been a religious sister, a Ph.D. candidate in theology at Fordham University at the time, and the kind of intellectual who could combine great common sense and an avid feminism with solidarity with the marginalized. We have been blessed as spiritual companions for 30 years.

Earliest Dreams Though this book is about selving, my essential self still eludes me, fading in and out like the misty northern lights we sometimes see around here at night. Perhaps I would call my self essentially a dreamer. All my earliest "work"—my life experience up to age twenty—culminated in the dream-come-true of joining the Jesuits. At age twenty, that's where I thought I would carve my niche. Jesuit spirituality thereafter became my spiritual style for twenty two years and even several years beyond.

Our Jesuit life was based on the ideal of modeling one's life on "Christ's," especially his poverty and solidarity with the oppressed, his chastity and celibacy, and his obedience to God—which we interpolated to mean obedience to our superiors and to the Holy Father in Rome. We embraced fully all the Church's means of supposedly growing in grace, most importantly meditation, ritual, reading and religious studies.

This spirituality also included imposing on ourselves physical hardships and penitential practices like scourging one's self several times a week and occasional fasting. Pleasure was usually to be avoided. Isolation from ordinary society was considered crucial in that early spirituality, and along with the asceticism came powerful illusions that our heroics made us inevitably superior to ordinary people (though we denied it). We could not see through the veil that covered over our growing egotism with its unspoken arrogance, its spiritual self-aggrandizement, its brute competitiveness and its wasted energies. We would have explained that we were becoming saintly, but in fact—in the warning words of a zen teacher, and unbeknownst to ourselves—some of us were nurturing a "giant-size ego." A giant-size ego is a heavy, heavy burden that, for many a cleric or ex-cleric, has to be carried throughout life.

It was at this time that I might say I put on my first mask, gradually assuming my first great acting role. Though Father Joseph Gschwend, my novice master, tried continuously to get me into the role of an Ignatius Loyola or a Francis Xavier, I secretly, compulsively, was becoming Bing Crosby. The song "Goin' My Way" still brings tears to my eyes, so important did it figure in my early motivations. I was good at singing, I could play the piano, I could act: Bing was my role model and the mask I donned. I couldn't help myself. We both looked great in a roman collar.

My next important work was to study, and that required heroics as well, filling a total of thirteen college-level years with books, papers, dramatics, music, liturgy, languages, meditations, disputations and above all—and most sweetly—conversations. We filled in all our non-study time with talk, and that more than anything else was my most satisfactory educational milieu. Finally ordained a priest in 1960, I soon left for the Korean missions, to teach English and music at Sogang University. These were years filled with excitement and creativity, and it was with regret that I returned three years later to an office in New York City to establish a central agency for Jesuit writers, located at the house where *America* magazine was published. I had been an assistant editor there for a year earlier on, and found my around-the-world move dramatic and invigorating, though I regretted setting aside my teaching role.

On-stage in Class   For six years of my Jesuit life, I was a classroom teacher. The teacher's role is a ritual one, so teachers also occasionally wear masks. My Jesuit teacher's mask carried an expression of authority, of infinite resourcefulness, of the expert with a humble manner, of the no-nonsense disciplinarian dressed in a long black robe. In this atmosphere of constant drama and physical exhaustion, my spirituality grew more humane. The six-plus long days of work each week brought me regularly to near physical exhaustion, and early on when I was missioned in South Dakota, I began to learn to be good to myself, to take a horse for a ride in the canyons, to find fascinating novels to read, to float comfortably for an hour in the world of Chopin and Beethoven. I could not brag after that of my no-pleasure asceticism, but there was lots to survive for, and I decided to survive.

Thus I learned how important it is to be less than perfect, to accept yourself as limited, as human. I began to admire and pay more attention to people who could simply enjoy life without feeling guilty. I began to rise each morning not only to save the world but to savor the world. My work life was shaping my spirituality. In each day's meditation I tried to see my day's work in its Teilhardian context: in how it "contributed to the unfolding of evolution " and to the world's "christification," as the great Jesuit visionary and paleontologist put it.

In 1968 once my Writers Agency task was done and handed over to others, instead of returning to Korea, I and a Jesuit friend dreamed up a film company, creating short discussion films for use in our American schools. The company floundered at first and then succeeded, and exists to this day though both the founders have long ago left the Jesuit Order. In 1972, now the father of two, I took a managerial job in a Washington, DC, bookstore, and three years later (after the store was held up five times) started my own in Vermont. The world of religious books enabled my wife and I to remain up to date in theology and spirituality, not to mention acquainting us with the new music that was coming alive within institutional Christianity—to which I dreamed of contributing.

My authentic self continued to blossom. During the Sandanista revolution in Nicaragua in the early '80's, three outstanding Catholic priests were given key governmental posts there—Foreign Minister, Minister of Culture, Minister of Education—and I dreamed up a whimsical song, then a 15-minute video, entitled "Padre Ernesto." The song dramatized the work of these priests and the great ideals of that revolution. I thought that music could constitute my contribution to the cause, but no such luck. People around me (my wife, for instance) were spending weeks and weeks in that Central American country, helping bring its idealistic dream to life. I found myself sucked into a cotton picking brigade, and in no time, I was flying south at the risk of my life.

I survived—barely—the heat and rodents in Nicaragua, but as I settled into my seat in an American Airlines plane jetting out of Miami after just two weeks picking cotton, I could not have been more exultant. Not only was I still alive, but three promising stars sparkled in my professional sky: my politico/religious song group had a Cleary-music gig in Los Angeles, opening for Judy Collins; I had a contract for a song album with the biggest religious music publisher in the U.S.; and the Asia Society had agreed verbally to stage my Korean musical off-off Broadway.

"Each mortal thing does one thing and the same: deals out that being indoors each one dwells, selves...." I felt at that moment that I was about to deal out my truest being, about to selve grandiloquently.

None of it happened. Over the next months each star fell from my sky in its own melancholy way. Why was this happening, I asked myself. And I answered: because death is part of everything living and everything that happens. Darkness edges every sky. Better to vote for the world we live in, the world as it is. And in the end my failures didn't really matter, for my primary self remained alive— though somewhat bruised—underneath.

And what is more, if Thomas Merton is right, there was/is a self in me even deeper than that which also survived. In *Conjectures of a Guilty Bystander*, Merton distinguishes helpfully between the false "self" ("The person I want myself to be...") and the true self ("At the center of our being is a point... which is untouched by sin ... which belongs entirely to God,... which is inaccessible to... our own mind.

...It is, so to speak, God's name written in us. ... It is like a pure diamond, blazing with the invisible light of heaven... . It is in everybody... .") Etty Hillesom helps here as well. In *An Interrupted Life*, she writes: "I carry on a sometimes silly, sometimes deadly serious, conversation with what is deepest and most central to my being, which for convenience sake I call God." What was deepest to my being felt firm.

For a full-figured dreamer like myself, this kind of brush with sobering disappointment is almost a pattern in my work life. My campaign song for candidate Geraldine Ferraro which cost several thousand dollars to make and six months to promote, got nowhere. My anti-drug film "Everybody's Goin' Where I've Been" went nowhere also, even after the U.S.Army said they loved it and began talking in the hundreds of thousands of dollars. The campaigns to prevent aid to the Contras, stop the Iraqi War, to aid the passing of the Equal Rights Amendment, all failed. Even Cliff Robertson's voice could not make a hit out of a little anti-war film, "Holy War". Despite all this, I have to admit with deep gratitude that more than a few dreams have come true.

The Great Scheme In the great scheme of things, my personal niche of belonging is modest, I believe. William Cleary belongs to that scheme mainly due to his being a dreamer with an active streak of inventiveness. "Through work one becomes conscious of who one really is," as Andrew Krivak puts it in this book's first chapter. The products of my creativity have not been world shaking ideas or stratospheric spiritual leadership, but most often just an elaboration on the philosophy and religion that have made up my ever-changing spirituality.

I think my chief claim to inventiveness has to do with what is called "prayer"—but that includes for me every kind of approach to the Divine Mystery itself, speaking into its silence, trying to feel comfortable with its darkness. My first book (*Facing God*, written in Korea) elaborated twenty different ways to spend time in meditation. (I was finding it hard to do.) My second book (*Hyphenated Priests*) predicted an end to professional "priests" who had no other profession but ministry; the book gave life-style accounts of a dozen priest-professionals—thus "hyphenated"—priest-lawyers, priest-professors, priest-scholars.

Next I became a hyphenated priest myself, a priest-filmmaker. I worked on just four films at that time, but one of them (*Me and the Monsters*) luckily hit just the right note for public schools, and has been used by them for twenty years. If I have made any significant mark on my milieu, it is through this 10-minute children's film on fear. At the time I made it, my personal life was changing dramatically as I was taking on a secular lifestyle. After I lost confidence in filmmaking (not knowing how successful it would eventually be), I began bookselling, a profession that occupied me for fifteen years. When I finally sold my store in 1985, I began to write and compose full time.

In a new burst of invention, I started with a version of the Book of Psalms on a computer disk, began "re-translating" them. This produced three books, each built on some of those re-translated psalms. The last of these I decorated with imaginary prayers by animals, in rhyming verse—and then it led to three other books containing more prayers by animals, bugs, fish and finally even vegetables. The truth is that I find it easy to figure out how almost any kind of critter should pray except myself.

Next, after stumbling on a magnificent study of the feminine in God, *She Who Is* by theologian Elizabeth Johnson, I composed a companion book called *Prayers To She Who Is*, which then spawned another, parallel book called *Prayers For Lovers*. Meanwhile, to while away the hours in airports, I began to versify Aesop's fables, then added off-beat spiritual practices for a book called *Prayers and Fables*. Now I'm into its volume two and web site uses.

Selving in Music   My musical work began with collaboration on original musical comedies for students in Jesuit schools and missions, and this climaxed with a musical play performed at the 1988 Olympics in Seoul, Korea, resurrected from a school play I had written when I was a teacher, twenty years earlier. Along the way I composed religious songs and settings for psalms which were useful in the rituals I was attending. Several albums of these were published by Credence Cassettes and other publishers, with another album of my "women's music" put out by the Women's Ordination Conference under the reverse-sexism pseudonym of Patience O'Neil.

Nowadays, at age 73, I labor on—with projects, like this present book, always awaiting attention in my works-in-progress studio. I am in there every day, eagerly selving away. Still, several times a month, at the Burlington Health and Rehabilitation Center, with 15 wheelchairs pulled up around my top-opened piano and my uncertain Irish tenor singing out "I'll Take You Home Again, Kathleen" or even "The Bells of St. Mary's" with other quavering voices all coming alive around me, Father Time gets stopped in his tracks and whisked back fifty, sixty, or seventy years. I feel at that moment that I am very deeply selving. I have almost become the Bing Crosby of my dreams, though now no longer dressed like Father O'Malley. It seems that, for that musical time-outside-of-time, trouble and pain all forgotten, memories are awakening again filled with romantic dreams, still alive in the land where anything's possible.

(*William Cleary is filmmaker, composer and author of several books of spirituality.*)

FINALE

It is interesting to look again at the Hopkins sonnet that provided the opening prelude of this book, including this time the closing six lines. It encompasses the Christian world-view laid out perhaps in its very finest paradigmatic image: that each Christian takes on the task of messianism, of "being for others,"—becomes a christ (a sentiment espoused as well by a rabbi friend of mine). As Krivak says in Chapter One: "(for the Christian) the dignity of work rests in its capacity to effect an imitation of Christ." While most of our contributors are at least culturally Christian, some are not—but all have contributed richly to this study because they have understood the lifelong task of selving as marked by a pattern of meaningfulness, however that would be expressed within their current world view. Here is, finally, the full Hopkins sonnet.

AS KINGFISHERS CATCH FIRE

As kingfishers catch fire, dragonflies draw flame,
   As tumbled over rim in roundy wells
   Stones ring; like each tucked string tells, each hung bell's
Bow swung finds tongue to fling out broad its name:
Each mortal thing does one thing and the same,
   Deals out that being indoors each one dwells:
   Selves—goes itself; myself it speaks and spells,
Crying *What I do is me: for that I came.* . . .

I say more: the just man justices,
Keeps grace, that keeps all his going graces,
Acts in God's eye what in God's eye he is:
Christ—for Christ plays in ten thousand places,
Lovely in limbs, and lovely in eyes not his
To the Father through the features of men's faces.

                                      1882

Finale

May we all frequently feel a touch of satisfaction in finding ourselves genuinely selving and crying *What I do is me, for that I came*, all this in harmony with whatever larger realities there are, within our common cloud of unknowing.

Finally, I am grateful more than I can say to each of the busy contributors to this book. The assignment was demanding, requiring serious thought, judgment, then discernment. But it was a labor of friendship, well worth the effort, I'm sure. I hope it was also a spiritual exercise that gave us each some enlightenment about ourselves, our *selves*, and our *selving*. In looking back this way, we each blow a kiss to the past surrendering to the futility of trying to judge it all, but trusting it was—like all expressions of friendship—never in vain.

William Cleary

Postscript

Honoring Eugene C. Bianchi

W.H. Auden, the late English poet, once spoke amusingly of his preference for honoring "the vertical man" rather than attending mostly to the horizontal. So it is a joy to be honoring Eugene Bianchi while he is yet vertical—but noting that he is much more than that. He is a monument of achievement.

When Gene and I were together at *America* magazine almost forty years ago, we all felt he was destined for great things but we were short on details. Did we dream he would write eight books? Hardly. Their titles are, in a way, a review of the concentrations of his very productive life. Here they are in reverse order, looking from the present time back toward his scholarly beginnings.

- *Elder Wisdom: Crafting Your Own Elderhood* (Crossroad 1994);
- *A Democratic Catholic Church* (with Rosemary Ruether) (Crossroad 1992);
- *On Growing Older* (Crossroad 1990);
- *Aging as a Spiritual Journey* (Crossroad 1982);
- *From Machismo to Mutuality* (with Rosemary Ruether) (Paulist 1976);
- *The Religious Experience of Revolutionaries* (Doubleday 1972);
- *Reconciliation* (Sheed 1969);
- *John XXIII and American Protestants* (Corpus 1968).

But this list gives us the merest sketch of Bianchi's long work life. He was also a classroom teacher for over thirty years, and that entailed thousands of lectures and students. What is even more interesting than all this—and more in keeping with the purport of this book—is his explorations of spirituality that lay behind the work, and constituted the background music for his scholarly career. Knowing he was to be the object of this *festschrift*, Gene agreed to put together a brief sketch of that spiritual journey. This is what he wrote.

How would I assess the interplay between my work life and my changing spirituality? Of course, I would have to first admit to whatever degree of self-deception goes into sizing up one's own inner development since knowing one's self is a life-long process. By spirituality I would mean the network of meaning and experience that seems to count most in interpreting the trajectory of my life. Another way of saying this is to ask about the motivating values energizing my life and work. My work experience for the last thirty-three years has been that of a college professor. Before that I spent a long time educating myself for the professorate and in preparing myself for service in the Jesuit order.

Four main shifts characterize this interfacing of my work and spirituality. First, I have moved from a more parochial, institutionalized understanding to a more personalized or individuated grasp of spirituality. Leaving the Jesuits, an order committed to Catholic teaching, launched this journey toward sitting loose to institutions. I have never thought that religious institutions were unimportant; like other social organizations, churches have valuable roles to play. The Civil Rights Movement, for instance, would not have happened the way it did without the churches.

But my work of intellectual inquiry into religious enterprises helped me see them as relative, historically-conditioned human inventions. Whitehead's process philosophy plus years of historical investigation into the origin of religions taught me that they are all always in the making, even if change seems glacially slow. Part of my learning process in this regard also stems from the ethos of the sixties which questioned all institutions. The lessening of institutional conformity led me to a greater interpersonal and inward focus in spirituality.

Second, Vatican II coincided with my theology studies in Louvain; both the Council and my teachers began the process of leading me to a more pluralistic spirituality. I would later characterize this spirituality as transtraditional, that is, living within a given tradition with greater porousness so that I could accept spiritual wisdom wherever it presented itself. I sometimes refer to this stance as catholic with a small "c." Doctoral study in a Protestant context gave me a concrete appreciation of religious thinking and practice beyond Catholicism. Later I would teach about Buddhism and discover it as both complement and antidote to religious ways ingrained in me since boyhood. Also Zen and the Tao Te Ching would help me rediscover meditation as a fruitful practice. Now, as a cosmopolitan catholic, I feel the tension of living with ambivalence and eclecticism in a tradition I once embraced as the clear and unique spiritual way.

Third, my explorations as a religion professor have brought me to a more metaphorical understanding of religious doctrine. Religious institutions are, of course, historical, but many of their teachings are not historical in the usual sense. For example, Christian teachings about incarnation and human redemption are figurative, faith-based interpretations about Jesus, a Jewish sage who in his lifetime preached much simpler tenets about the domain of God. Early Christians, especially their brightest leaders, developed the Christian religion with its full-blown doctrines about God and humans. This great religious construction flowed from Christian theological imagination and experience. It was and is a metaphorical enterprise linked to the historical institution of the church. These major doctrines, not to be confused with ethical teachings, are themselves metaphorical, poetic attempts to fashion wider meaning and direction in life.

I see all religions including modern ones in this light. This metaphorical, religious poetry, its doctrines (sometimes orchestrated liturgically), are part of the humanistic project of understanding perennial questions that challenge our species.

Finally, my spirituality has become more nature-oriented or ecological. It is harder to parse the causes of this development. Here I need to think of my work in a broader sense, to include my ordinary life. Movement to a more earthly spirituality in recent years derives from my growing day-to-day awareness of ecological problems which translated into a course on ecology and religion.

But there are two other work-related happenings that brought me down to earth, as it were. One is the aging process which reminds me about the seasons of life, the ephemeral beauty of existence, and about my place and purpose as a creature of earth. Another "work" that influenced my spirituality has been my ups and downs with relationships. It has been a long learning curve that pulled the abstract academic out of the clouds and down to terra firma.

In sum, I look back at my path as a journey in four stages, and my teaching and publications seem to be stations and pauses at plateaus along the way, helping me see where I have been, and how I became who I am today, a slightly fatigued but still lively traveler.

Eugene Bianchi's traveling continues . He is presently working on a national study of Jesuits and former Jesuits in the United States. Another of his interests is trans-traditional spirituality or the effort for a more worldwide religious ecumenism. His teaching at Emory University has included a course on ecology and religion, which studies ecological spirituality from both eastern and western perspectives and he has published a number of articles on ecological spirituality. He was the first coordinator of the religion and ecology group in the American Academy of Religion.

With his wife, Dr. Margaret Herrman, a professional mediator and scholar in conflict resolution at the University of Georgia, he now makes his home in Athens, Georgia.

If there is some truth in the modern contention that "the basic unit of spirituality is no longer the individual, but relationship" (Zappone), then the present volume adds an important documentation of Gene Bianchi's spirituality. Though there is joy in selving, that is only part of human blossoming: there is also the strong web of life that is our friendships and intellectual links to others—and this volume is now a part of that testimony and substance. May it also be a source of joy to our friend in his retirement, and a useful tool for further thinking and linking.

William Cleary

Winter 1999